DATE DUE

GAYLORD			PRINTED IN U.S.A

THE RELIGION OF DR JOHNSON
AND OTHER ESSAYS

The Rev. WILLIAM THOMAS CAIRNS, D. D. *d, 1944-*

The Religion of
DR JOHNSON

and Other Essays

Essay Index Reprint Series

BOOKS FOR LIBRARIES PRESS
FREEPORT, NEW YORK

STANDARD BOOK NUMBER:

8369-1279-9

LIBRARY OF CONGRESS CATALOG CARD NUMBER:

71-93324

PRINTED IN THE UNITED STATES OF AMERICA

CONTENTS

CONTENTS

INTRODUCTION

THE author of these essays was a well-known minister of the Scottish Church. During the first thirty-three years of his life there were three main branches of that Church. In 1900 two of them united, and in 1929 the one thus formed and the other from which at different times its component parts had broken away, came auspiciously together to reconstitute in a happy unity the historic Church of Scotland.

To the smallest of the three sections thus reunited—the United Presbyterian, itself composed in 1847 by the union of the Secession and Relief Churches—William Cairns belonged. He bore a name of high honour in that section, and indeed throughout Scotland. In the present writer's youth there were in the ministry of what was currently called in brief the U.P. Church, no more markworthy or venerated figures than those of David Cairns of Stitchel, in Berwickshire, not far from the Border, and John Cairns, D.D., LL.D., Professor of Theology and Principal in the College of the Church. The two brothers were so much alike that the sight of one immediately suggested the other. Especially in their later years they would have attracted attention in any gathering, by their tall, massive, stooping figures, by the snow-white hair framing their striking faces and flowing down upon their shoulders, and by their retention, in their ordinary dress, of the swallow-tailed broadcloth coat and the dignified old-style stock which their younger contemporaries had long forsaken for newer fashions. A deep Christian humility characterized both men and was evident in their habitual bearing. There could be no more remarkable instance of this than John's refusal of nomination for the Principalship of the University of Edinburgh because he would allow no inducement to turn him aside from his complete self-dedication to the service of his Church, and his successful concealment, even from the members of his family, of the great opportunity so offered him, until, after his death, his biographer, Professor A. R. MacEwen, found the incontestable proof of it among his papers.

There were three sons of the Stitchel manse. Brought up

under the large-minded and liberating influence of their father, and of a mother not less distinctive and decisive in the impress made by her upon their characters, it was natural that each of them, in his own way, came to distinction. John Cairns of Dumfries, the eldest, was a scholar of wide and varied learning, a pioneer in the ecumenical movement, and the author of a short but excellent Life of his uncle, the Principal, in the *Famous Scots* series. The second brother, David S. Cairns, is widely known as the author of works which have given him a name of high repute among theologians and ministers on both sides of the Atlantic, and as Principal for many years of what is now known as Christ's College, the theological seminary of the University of Aberdeen.

On their mother's side, the three brothers were scions of the notable 'dynasty' founded by John Brown of Haddington (1722-1787), whose *Self-Interpreting Bible* invested his name in his own time and for long afterwards, with a fame far out-reaching that which gave him pre-eminence in his own (Secession) branch of the Church. The record of this remark-able family may be found in the *Letter to John Cairns, D.D.*, which appears in vol. ii of the *Horae Subsecivae* of the Dr John Brown whose *Rab and his Friends*, *Pet Marjorie*, *Jeems the Door-keeper*, and other papers rich in the charm of a rare personality, have a secure place among minor Scottish classics. The *Letter* itself was written as a kind of intimate postscript or "supple-mentary chapter" to Principal Cairns's Memoir of the author's father, Dr John Brown of Broughton Place, Edinburgh (1784-1858), one of the most eminent divines and Church leaders of his time, and is in its own kind a veritable master-piece of unconventional biography.

William T. Cairns, the third son of the Stitchel manse, having on both sides family connections of such distinction, deep-rooted all of them in the soil of the Church they loved, could hardly fail to gravitate naturally towards the work of the Christian ministry. His preparation for it gave no sign of exceptional equipment for it. Though always intelligent and varied in his mental interests, he achieved no distinction either at the University of Edinburgh or at the Theological

Hall of his own Church. He was an ardent member of the Philomathic Society at the University, and zealously availed himself of Professor Henry Drummond's Sunday evening meetings for students; but though diligent in his studies, his mind remained unkindled by any of the subjects of the then hard-and-fast curriculum. Like many other students of unquestioned mental powers, he found Mathematics a field of study so uncongenial and hard to cultivate that he had ruefully to describe himself as *bis aratus* before the examiners passed him for the M.A. degree. Intellectually his development was slow, and as yet there was little sign of the breadth of humane culture which his University ultimately recognized by conferring on him, *honoris causa*, its doctorate of Divinity.

When he entered upon the period of probation which is in the Scottish Church the avenue to the regular ministry, he exhibited none of the showy gifts by which congregations are apt to be most readily attracted. Nor did he, then or ever, cultivate any of the arts of popular appeal by which men of far inferior quality among his contemporaries made their way before him into charges of their own. But a sphere after his own heart awaited him. In 1896 he was called to Abernethy, in southern Perthshire, a district rich in historical associations as well as natural beauty. His imagination could not fail to be quickened by the constant sight of the Pictish tower, one of the few perfect examples still existing, which dominates the village. Hardly less could his historical sense be appealed to by the fact that the congregation which called him to be its minister cherished proudly its own tradition as one of the first five congregations to constitute, in 1733, the Secession Church to which his ancestry belonged. Another association deeply touched his family sentiment; for it was in that congregation, in its early days, that 'the "heroic" old man of Haddington' from whom part of his own blood was derived, heard in his youth his call to the ministry, and began to develop the gifts which in after years were to bear such rich and far-spread fruits.

Twelve idyllic years were spent in Abernethy. To the manse there he brought from Sutherland his wife, to whom this book is dedicated. Ably practical, as the daughter of a Highland manse could hardly fail to be, she was gifted, cultivated, sensitive, intellectually alive to her husband's interests while finding time to pursue her own. The happiness of his home-life was not the least of the stimulative influences that set in motion the intellectual development which went on from that point to the end.

From his ultimately richly furnished bookshelves it was easy to deduce what interests were dominant with him. Theology of course was prominent; history and biography were copiously represented; geography, somewhat curiously, had an unfailing fascination for him, so that he was able to gather from his stores for friends setting out for countries he was never himself to see, maps and the best of the relevant literature: the present writer remembers well how abundantly he was thus supplied alike for the Near East and for the great new countries of the West. In general literature he ranged far and wide, and read voraciously, besides, in the great Libraries of Edinburgh.

Of pictures he was fond, and had a sound judgement; and music was a perennial fountain of pleasure to him.

The devoutness of his mind may be inferred from the fact that he made it a matter of daily discipline to read a chapter of the Old Testament in Hebrew every morning, and one from the New in Greek every night.

On his retiral from the active ministry he returned to the Latin classics with renewed and intensified interest, and to the Waverley Novels, which, he being himself a son of the Scott country, had informed and inspired his youth. In the poetry, history, and legendry of the Borderland his mind was steeped. It is suggestive that when he entered the Nursing Home where the last call was to come to him, the books he chose to be the companions of his solitude were a Greek Testament, the Golden Treasury selection from Wordsworth, and the Prayer Book of the Scottish Episcopal Church. These afford evidence enough, not only of a liberally educated but of a deeply spiritual mind.

The Abernethy period was brought to an end in 1908 by a call to Edinburgh. All his life, he once remarked, had been

spent in small churches. Davidson Church, Eyre Place, like
Abernethy, answered that description. At that time, too, it
presented difficulties which uncommon courage was needed to
face and overcome. In that restricted sphere the rest of his
fruitful ministry was spent. His early preaching, always con-
scientious and thoughtful, suffered somewhat from his bondage
to "the paper"; but as time went on it deepened and grew
richer till one good judge declared it to be the best in Edinburgh. At the same time it always tended to lack freedom and
to make its appeal mainly to the more thoughtful and dis-
cerning people in the pews. One of these once, in a mood of
affectionate exasperation, cried *ex animo*, "Oh, if he would only
preach as he can sing!" If, however, the consequence was some
limitation of his influence from the pulpit, there was a com-
pensating advantage in the field of his ministry not being too
extended. He had a strong pastoral instinct, and an intense
interest in human beings, a faculty also of getting easily on
friendly and easy terms with them; thus his people came to
know the riches of his mind and heart so well that they gave
him something more than the loyalty and esteem which are
everywhere the reward of assiduous and devoted service; they
gave him the warmer response evoked by a character and spirit
whose quality needs to be seen at close quarters to be fully
valued, and which intimately to know was inevitably to love.

Certain outside interests also contributed to the development
of his gifts. He enjoyed the society of his fellows, and gave
liberally of his time and thought to certain administrative
Committees of the General Assembly of his Church. For many
years he was a member and secretary of the Edinburgh Theological Society, a distinguished fraternity of expert theologians.
From the papers he contributed to its proceedings it was
tempting to select for this volume a few of a specifically
theological character; but it was decided to restrict the choice
to papers that would appeal to a wider circle of his friends.

From his youth up one of his ruling interests was Hymnology.
It commended itself to him the more because he was himself a
singer, gifted with a noble voice, of unusual range and purity
and power. For many years he acted as honorary precentor of

the Presbytery of Edinburgh. Naturally, therefore, his scholarship included the musical as well as the literary and historical
aspects of hymnody. No member of the Committee which
edited the *Revised Church Hymnary* made a more all-round
contribution to its excellences than he. To the *Handbook to the
Church Hymnary* he contributed the historical notes on the
hymns from No. 300 onwards. The Edinburgh Society of
Organists numbered him among its most honoured members.
And when the Hymn Society of Great Britain and Ireland was
formed, it was in the order of necessity that he should be one of
the small group of its founders, one of the most trusted and
sagacious of its counsellors, and a frequent contributor of
articles of value to its quarterly Bulletin.

The essays in this volume were all written for one or another
of the Societies of which he was a member. Readers should
keep in mind that they represent the mere *parerga*, the secondary products of the industry, of a busy city minister. They
were not intended for publication. Two of them *were* published
in the last years of his life in response to the insistent demand of
those who heard them read: the one on *The Religion of Dr
Johnson* is here included by permission of the Editorial Committee of *The Evangelical Quarterly*, and that on *The Constituents
of a Good Hymn*, first read to a Conference of the Hymn Society
in King's College, Cambridge, is reprinted from an Occasional
Paper of that Society. Apart from these, none of the essays had
the benefit of the author's reconsideration and revision. This
fact will explain and, it is hoped, condone, whatever faults may
be found in them; but, possible deficiencies notwithstanding,
his friends have felt that the essays ought to be published, alike
for the interest of their subjects, and as reflections of a mind
and spirit of an unusually attractive quality.

Yet through any such medium it is impossible that the
personality of the author should transmit the warmth of friendliness which all who knew him were quick to feel. His con-
victions were strong; he was not without his prejudices; and he
could use trenchant and salty speech in the expression of them
as need demanded; but his essentially kindly and irenical

spirit made it impossible for him ever to make an enemy: on the contrary, it made for him hosts of friends.

As to this, let the last word be said by the Editor of *Life and Work*, the organ of the Church of Scotland, in a farewell tribute: 'Was there in the Church of Scotland a more widely or warmly loved man than Dr W. T. Cairns? One doubts it. He was a man of rare gifts. . . But he was as devoid of personal ambition as a man could well be, pursuing his interests for their own sake, and serving his flock and his Church out of sheer affection and the loyalty of his heart. He brought with him at all times a warmth that will linger in the hearts of those who knew him; and, as a colleague has written, "The place where he has been and laboured will long be radiant with afterglow." '

Edinburgh. November, 1945.

THE RELIGION OF DOCTOR JOHNSON

I

'Doctor Johnson, the most abnormally English Creature
God ever made.'[1]

SUCH is the pronouncement of the present Master of
Trinity, Dr George Macaulay Trevelyan—himself in the
front rank of modern historians, and surpassed only by
kinsmen even more illustrious: his father Sir George Otto Trevelyan, and his great-uncle Lord Macaulay. Magisterial and
unqualified as the verdict is, is it justified? Johnson as Boswell
saw and described him for all time seems at first little more
than a bundle of contradictions: formidable, irascible, almost
incredibly and unendurably rude at times, prejudiced to the
last degree, yet possessing a wonderful insight into the heart of
men and things, a power almost equally wonderful of describing what he saw, and, withal, a tender and unwearied charity
to all weak and broken creatures. 'He is now become miser-
able,' said Goldsmith of a man who bore a very bad character,
'and that insures the protection of Johnson.' The Johnson of
Mrs Thrale, of Fanny Burney, of Hannah More, of Sir John
Hawkins—'Sir John, Sir, is a very *unclubable* man'—of Sir
Joshua Reynolds: how different each portrait is from all
the others! Yet in each and all of them there is something
extraordinarily real, no mere Brocken Spectre looming up
through mountain mists menacing and gigantic, but a man
fundamentally simple, lovable, sincere. Underlying all surface contradictions was a religion which he was never ashamed
to confess, unifying all the diverse elements of his character,
straightening what he himself would have called its *anfrac-
tuosities*, overcoming disabilities under which almost every
other man would have sunk—partial blindness, overpowering
melancholy, almost constant pain—and giving peace at the
last.

The contrasts and contradictions are on the surface, and are

[1] "The Age of Johnson" in A. S. Turberville's *Johnson's England*, Vol. 1,
p. 6.

very much what one sees in the age in which he lived. Johnson was pre-eminently a child of the eighteenth century, and one can no more imagine him away from the England of that epoch with all its glories and its limitations than one can think of Luther away from the Germany of the first half of the sixteenth. The eighteenth century has been called 'The Age of Enlightenment', and deserves the proud title. But darkness fought hard, and wherever one looked, life was full of the most glaring contrasts. The finest manner and the rudest and coarsest manners were to be seen in one person. Luxury and squalor jostled each other in the same room. One remembers Sans Souci, the palace of Frederick the Great: the lofty and beautifully-proportioned bedrooms all gilded wherever gold leaf could be stuck on wall and ceiling, chairs and tables and couches unmatched for elegance of design and artistic craftsmanship, and—the most meagre provision for washing, in the tiniest of basins and ewers.

Conditions were little—if at all—better in England. A wave of prosperity was sweeping over the country. With Clive in India and Wolfe at Quebec and Hawke at Quiberon Bay,

> To add something new to this wonderful year

(1759), when, as Macaulay says, 'every month had its illuminations and bonfires and every wind brought some messenger charged with joyful tidings and hostile standards', England was experiencing the thrill and exhilaration of the spacious days of Queen Elizabeth.[1] But, among gentle and simple alike, there was a strange torpor of the higher faculties, and the general ignorance of, and indifference to, spiritual considerations almost pass belief. Bishop Butler's sombre verdict a quarter of a century before was still very largely justified:

[1] Reference may be permitted to a still more widely-known event, obscure and unheralded at the time, when on 25 January 1759, in an 'auld clay biggin' at Alloway near Ayr,

> Our monarch's hindmost year but ane
> Was five and twenty days begun,
> 'Twas then a blast o' Janwar win'
> Blew hansel in on Robin.

'It is come, I know not how, to be taken for granted, by many persons, that Christianity is not so much as a subject of inquiry; but that it is, now at length, discovered to be fictitious. And accordingly they treat it, as if, in the present age, this were an agreed point among all people of discernment; and nothing remained, but to set it up as a principal subject of mirth and ridicule, as it were by way of reprisals, for its having so long interrupted the pleasures of the world.'[1]

But the tide was beginning to turn. The Spirit of God was moving on the face of the waters. John Wesley in his apostolic journeys from the Isles of Scilly to Inverness, Charles Wesley pouring out hymns by the thousand, Whitefield in the crowded Moorfields Tabernacle, and, hardly less potent, Johnson in The Club and through his writings, were each and all setting men's thoughts astir, and preparing the way for a revolution as far-reaching as, and infinitely more beneficent than, that in France before the century ended. Barrier after barrier long supposed insurmountable fell, the last and stiffest of all being that which was within, deeply entrenched—the strange, typically eighteenth-century dislike and dread of 'Enthusiasm'. One recalls Hume, flinging to the winds all native inhibitions of speech, as he declaims against 'the frantic madman delivering himself over, blindly and without reserve, to the supposed illapses of the Spirit, and to inspiration from above', and Johnson himself in his definition of enthusiasm in the *Dictionary*, as 'A vain confidence of divine favour or communication'.

II

Samuel Johnson was born at Lichfield on 18 September 1709 in a house at the corner of Market Street almost under the shadow of the Cathedral with its lovely three spires—the 'Ladies of the Vale'. He was handicapped from birth, scrofula, St Vitus' Dance, and partial blindness leaving him scarcely a day without pain throughout the seventy-five years of his life. Over and above the physical disability, he inherited from his father a deep-rooted and inveterate

---

[1] Advertisement to first Edition of *The Analogy of Religion.*

melancholy, the black days of which made life a burden, taking away all power of work, and haunting him with the dread of madness practically to the end. When one remembers this, one ceases to wonder at, or to be repelled by, the morbidity which is the constant background of the *Prayers and Meditations*, or the sombre outlook on life in many of the essays in *The Rambler*. The marvel is that Johnson was able to accomplish so much, and that by far the greater part of his work was, in both thought and expression, of so noble a quality.

Like so many other English children, then and since, he was taught the Collects by heart, a single reading being enough to enable his vice-like memory to retain the great simple cadences for the rest of his life. He never wished to get away from the Collect form. 'I know of no good prayers but those in the Book of Common Prayer,' he once said to his old college friend Dr Adams. 'I will not compose prayers for you, Sir, because you can do it for yourself.' 'Sunday was a heavy day with me when I was a boy. My mother confined me on that day, and made me read *The Whole Duty of Man*, from a great part of which I could derive no instruction.'

A lonely, unhappy boyhood, shut off as he was by his physical ailments from association with all but a very few of the Lichfield boys of his own age, was followed by a lonely residence in Oxford, where he read extensively through the greater part of Classical Literature, and was 'depressed by poverty and irritated by disease'.[1] It was then that he chanced to fall in with William Law's *Serious Call to a Devout and Holy Life*, that famous little book which has so strongly influenced readers of the most diverse types. 'I expected to find it a dull

[1] In an interesting article in *The London Quarterly and Holborn Review* for July 1943 on 'The Influence of John Wesley on Johnson's Religion', Mr Harry Belshaw proves that Johnson was in residence at Pembroke when Wesley returned to Oxford and resumed his duties as fellow and tutor of Lincoln. But that the two men met at that time, and began the friendship which later was to ripen into something very warm and appreciative, though always with a strong critical element, remains unproved, and I think, despite Mr Belshaw's ingenious arguments, not very probable.

book (as such books generally are), and perhaps to laugh at it. But I found Law quite an overmatch for me; and this was the first occasion of my thinking in earnest of religion after I became capable of rational inquiry.' Whether Law was the best kind of spiritual physician for a man like Johnson may well be doubted. The two men were very different, united only in their keen interest in human nature, and perhaps even more in their common love of argument. When the heat of battle was on him, Johnson would 'talk for victory', quite regardless of any other consideration. But there was nothing in him of the self-conscious, self-admiring cleverness—'cleverality', to borrow a word of Charlotte Brontë's—which mars even the best of Law's work. 'Johnson,' says Canon Overton, 'in spite of his ruggedness, was full of *bonhomie:* he took a broader view of life than Law did; he thought the world was to be leavened, not renounced, by the Christian; and thus he was able to extend his influence over a far wider area during his life-time, and to leave works behind him which would be read by a far wider class of readers after his death than Law did.'[1]

We have no detailed consecutive narrative in which it is possible to trace the rise and progress of religion in his soul. It was no part of his manly objective nature to feel very much interested in his own mental states and feelings, still less to cherish a thought of self-pity, and, least of all, to lay bare before the curious gaze of others 'the pageant of his bleeding heart'. Johnson was no day-to-day journal-keeper, like Macaulay or Scott, still less like Pepys. 'Most men', he once said to that inveterate diarist Mrs Thrale, 'have their bright and their cloudy days; at least, they have days when they put their powers into act, and days when they suffer them to repose.' In place of any such *Journal Intime*, we have the *Prayers and Meditations*, entries made from time to time between his twenty-ninth birthday, 18 September 1738, and his seventy-fifth, 1784. When first written they were never intended for any purpose but his own private use, and many of his friends after his death were greatly shocked by the indiscreet publicity given to them by the Editor, Dr Strahan,

[1] *Life and Opinions of William Law*, p. 60.

Vicar of Islington, to whom he had handed the manuscript. There is very little in them of the so-called *Johnsonese*: the Latinized forms and balanced antitheses characteristic of the *Rambler* or *Idler* essays, or *Rasselas*. There is nothing at all of the self-conscious 'fine writing' which too often intrudes itself into many modern carefully composed prayers. Rather, as Augustine Birrell finely says: 'In these *Prayers and Meditations* the reader is admitted—let him not abuse the occasion— into the innermost sanctuary of a soul. It is a welcome retreat. . . . Doctor Johnson's trembling piety and utter sincerity is a true haven of refuge.'

Certain days he was accustomed to keep with fixed religious observances: Good Friday, Easter, his birthday (18 September), and the day on which his wife died (28 March). The prayers in connection with this last anniversary are almost too poignant for quotation, but the sorrow is always that of a strong man, without a trace of exhibitionism. There is one very characteristic touch under the entry, Good Friday, 28 March 1777—twenty-five years after the blow fell that 'had almost broke my heart': 'I remembered that it was my wife's dying day, and begged pardon for all our sins, and commended her: but resolved to mix little of my own sorrows or cares with the great solemnity.'[1]

There are long gaps in the series—the longest being six years. Then, when he hears of the death of some old friend, or starts on a journey, or is bidding farewell to Streatham Park which had been more than a home to him for so many years, the entries become frequent. As we read them, we begin to understand what it was in Johnson that won him the reverence —and, if you like, the forbearance—of the brilliant coterie of which he was the acknowledged centre: masters in their own professions like Burke and Reynolds, Goldsmith and Garrick; disciples like Mrs Thrale, and Hannah More, and Fanny Burney; rakes and scoffers like Beauclerk and Wilkes—not to speak of Boswell, who, in a manner all his own, exemplified the characteristics of all three classes.

Johnson of The Club we may come to know very intimately.

[1] *Prayers and Meditations*, p. 151.

But Johnson the Grub Street bookseller's hack, heart-sick with hope deferred, lonely, poverty-stricken and often dinnerless, tramping London Streets all night with wastrels like Richard Savage because neither could muster the coppers to pay for a lodging, we find it hard to visualize. Here is one of the prayers dating from that dim period:

'January 1st, 1744. Almighty and Everlasting God, in whose hands are Life and Death, by whose Will all things were created, and by whose Providence they are sustained, I return Thee thanks that Thou hast given me Life, and that Thou hast continued it to this time; that Thou hast hitherto forborn to snatch me away in the midst of Sin and Folly, and hast permitted me still to enjoy the means of Grace, and vouchsafed to call me yet again to Repentance. Grant, O merciful Lord, that Thy Call may not be in vain: that my Life may not be continued to increase my Guilt, and that Thy gracious Forbearance may not harden my heart in wickedness. Let me remember, O my God, that as Days and Years pass over me, I approach nearer to the grave where there is no repentance; and grant, that by the assistance of Thy Holy Spirit, I may so pass through this Life, that I may obtain Life everlasting, for the sake of our Lord Jesus Christ. Amen.'[1]

Again, we have the prayer on the day of his mother's funeral, 23 January 1759, when he was in London, unable to travel to Lichfield. A few days previously he had written her a very beautiful and touching letter: 'You have been the best mother and I believe the best woman in the world. I thank you for your indulgence to me, and beg forgiveness of all that I have done ill and all that I have omitted to do well.'

'Almighty God, merciful Father, in whose hands are life and death, sanctify unto me the sorrow which I now feel. Forgive me whatever I have done unkindly to my mother, and whatever I have omitted to do kindly. Make me to remember her good precepts and good example, and to reform my life according to Thy holy word, that I may lose no more opportunities of good. I am sorrowful, O Lord; let not my sorrow be without fruit. Let it be followed by holy resolutions, and lasting

[1] Op. cit. p. 4.

amendment, that, when I shall die like my mother, I may be received to everlasting life.

'I commend, O Lord, so far as it may be lawful, into Thy hands, the soul of my departed mother, beseeching Thee to grant her whatever is most beneficial to her in her present state . . . And, O Lord, grant unto me that am now about to return to the common comforts and business of the world, such moderation in all enjoyments, such diligence in honest labour, and such purity of mind, that, amid all the changes, miseries, or pleasures of life, I may keep my mind fixed upon Thee, and improve every day in grace, till I shall be received into Thy Kingdom of Eternal happiness.'[1]

There may be something old-fashioned, and even remote, in the feeling and the expression so firmly controlled, but how sincere it all is, how manly, how tender!

Another extract from the *Prayers and Meditations* is well known, and it shows, as perhaps we see nowhere else, the very heart of the thunderous autocrat.

'Sunday, Oct. 18, 1767. Yesterday, Oct. 17, at about ten in the morning, I took my leave for ever of my dear old friend, Catherine Chambers, who came to live with my mother about 1724 and has been but little parted from us since. She buried my father, my brother, and my mother. She is now fifty-eight years old.

'I desired all to withdraw, then told her that we were to part for ever; that as Christians, we should part with prayer; and that I would, if she was willing, say a short prayer beside her. She expressed great desire to hear me; and held up her poor hands, as she lay in bed, with great fervour, while I prayed kneeling by her, nearly in the following words: Almighty and most merciful Father, whose loving-kindness is over all Thy works, behold, visit, and relieve this Thy servant, who is grieved with sickness. Grant that the sense of her weakness may add strength to her faith, and seriousness to her repentance. And grant that by the help of Thy Holy Spirit, after the pains and labours of this short life, we may all obtain everlasting happiness, through Jesus Christ our Lord: for whose sake hear our prayers. Amen. Our Father . . .

'I then kissed her. She told me that to part was the greatest

---

[1] Op. cit. p. 36.

pain that she had ever felt, and that she hoped we should meet again in a better place. I expressed, with swelled eyes, and great emotion of tenderness, the same hopes. We kissed, and parted, I humbly hope to meet again, and to part no more.'[1]

III

One part of the book which, on its publication after Johnson's death, raised a considerable amount of feeling and even scandal, was that revealing the morbid scrutiny to which he subjected himself, more especially in his preparation for Easter Communion. There are whole pages of lamentations, of whose sincerity there can be no doubt, over his own slackness in church attendance, Bible reading, study of the Christian religion, and sluggishness in getting out of bed in the morning. This last was an almost life-long trial to him, and again and again we have resolves noted: 'To rise at eight, or as soon as I can', mingled with acknowledgements that 'When I was up, I have indeed done but little: yet it is no slight advancement to obtain for so many hours more the consciousness of being.' More often we have only very humble and repeated confessions of complete failure, either in this respect, or in weightier matters, or again in what his scrupulosity considered the sin of breaking some Church fast by eating hot-cross buns or drinking coffee with Mr Thrale. No doubt this has its ludicrous side, and it certainly gave occasion for creatures like John Courtenay in his *Poetical Review of the Literary and Moral Character of Dr Samuel Johnson* to write:

> On Tetty's[2] state his frighted fancy runs,
> And Heaven's appeas'd by Cross unbutter'd buns:
> He sleeps and fasts, pens on himself a libel,
> And still believes, but never reads the Bible.

One who might have known better, and ought to have had more sympathy with souls in distress, William Cowper, allowed himself to write to John Newton (17 August 1785):

'His prayers for the dead and his minute account of the rigour

[1] Op. cit. pp. 76f.
[2] His dead wife.

with which he observed Church fasts, whether he drank tea or
coffee, whether with sugar or without, and whether one or two
dishes of either, are the most important items to be found in
this childish register of the great Johnson, supreme dictator in
the chair of literature, and almost a driveller in his closet; a
melancholy witness to testify how much of the wisdom of this
world may consist with almost infantine ignorance of the
affairs of a better.'

And again, a few days later, to William Unwin (27 August
1785):

'Had he studied his Bible more, to which by his own confession he was in great part a stranger, he had known better what
use to make of his retired hours, and had trifled less. His lucu-
brations of this sort have rather the appearance of religious
dotage, than of any vigorous exertions towards God. It will be
well if the publication prove not hurtful in its effects by exposing the best cause, already too much despised, to ridicule still
more profane.'

Here we see that curious callousness of the eighteenth century which one catches even, at times, in Cowper, who had a
certain feline streak in him, and which was to be seen side by
side with excessive rancid sentimentality, as in page after
page of the odious Laurence Sterne. The present-day reader,
at any rate, has nothing but profound respect for Johnson
looking over these old papers with their long past resolutions:

'I think I was ashamed or grieved to find how long and how
often I had resolved what yet, except for about one half year,
I have never done. My nights are now such as give me no quiet
rest; whether I have not lived resolving till the possibility of
performance is past, I know not. God help me, I will yet try.'[1]

It must again be emphasized that these memoranda were
intended in the first instance for the writer's eyes alone. Like
Carlyle, a century later, he was willing to give to would-be
biographers such information as they needed, but he probably
never dreamed of these often broken sentences being literally
transcribed. Few can have guessed at the existence of such a

[1] *Prayers and Meditations*, p. 129.

record, and fewer still can have seen it during the author's
lifetime. In any case, there is very little in its point of view and
trend of thought different from the massive and sombre
philosophy of life sketched in *The Rambler*, *The Idler*, and
Rasselas, or in such a poem, 'grave, masculine, and strong'—to
quote Cowper's tribute—as *The Vanity of Human Wishes*.

> Where then shall Hope and Fear their objects find?
> Must dull Suspence corrupt the stagnant mind?
> Must helpless man, in ignorance sedate,
> Roll darkling down the torrent of his fate?
> Must no dislike alarm, no wishes rise,
> No cries attempt the mercies of the skies?
> Inquirer, cease: petitions yet remain,
> Which Heav'n may hear, nor deem Religion vain.
> Still raise for good the supplicating voice,
> But leave to Heav'n the Measure and the Choice . . .
> Pour forth thy fervours for a healthful mind,
> Obedient passions, and a will resign'd;
> For love, which scarce Collective Man can fill;
> For patience, sov'reign o'er transmuted ill;
> For faith, that, panting for a happier seat,
> Counts death kind Nature's signal of retreat;
> These goods for man, the laws of Heav'n ordain,
> These goods He grants, who grants the pow'r to gain;
> With these Celestial Wisdom calms the mind,
> And makes the happiness she does not find.

One famous passage in *The Idler*[1]—strangely misnamed—
written immediately after the death of his mother, gives
Johnson's mature and considered conclusions. He has been
speaking—not unworthily—of death, and the effect which it
has on the survivors.

'These are the great occasions which force the mind to take
refuge in Religion; when we have no help in ourselves, what
can remain but that we look up to a higher and a greater
Power? and to what hope may we not raise our eyes and hearts,
when we consider that the greatest power is the best? . . .
'The precepts of *Epictetus*, who teaches us to endure what
the Laws of the Universe make necessary, may silence, but not

[1] No. 41.

content us. The dictates of *Zeno*, who commands us to look with indifference on external things, may dispose us to conceal our sorrow, but cannot assuage it. Real alleviation of the loss of friends, and rational tranquillity in the prospect of our own dissolution, can be received only from the promises of Him in whose hands are life and death, and from the assurance of another and better state, in which all tears will be wiped from the eyes, and the whole soul shall be filled with joy. Philosophy may infuse stubbornness, but Religion only can give Patience.'

In passages like these it is possible to see how closely the writer keeps to the subject of his discourse, patiently and persistently hammering out the expression of his thought till at last he makes it say exactly what he wishes to say, no more but no less. It is this moral weight which gives momentum to all Johnson's judgements, arbitrary and prejudiced though they often are. If he was impatient to the verge of rudeness—and beyond it—with what he called 'cant' in other people, it was because he was persistently laying violent hands on the hateful thing in his own mind, which must be cleared from it at all costs.

'To Johnson [says Carlyle] as compared with Hume, Life was as a Prison, to be endured with heroic faith: to Hume it was little more than a foolish Bartholomew-Fair Show-booth, with the foolish crowdings and elbowings of which it was not worth while to quarrel; the whole would break up, and be at liberty, so *soon*. Both realized the highest Task of Manhood, that of living like men; each died not unfitly, in his way: Hume as one, with factitious, half-false gayety, taking leave of what was itself wholly but a lie: Johnson as one, with awe-struck yet resolute and piously expectant heart, taking leave of a Reality, to enter a Reality still higher.'[1]

'I told him [said Boswell once] that David Hume said to me he was no more uneasy to think he should *not be* after his life, than that he *had not been* before he began to exist. Johnson: "Sir, if he really thinks so, his perceptions are disturbed; he is mad; if he does not think so, he lies. He may tell you he holds his finger in the flame of a candle without feeling pain: would you believe him? When he dies, he at least gives up all he has". . . .

[1] *Essay on Johnson.*

To my question whether we might not fortify our minds for the
approach of death, he answered in a passion, "No, Sir, let it
alone. It matters not how a man dies, but how he lives. The
act of dying is not of importance, it lasts so short a time. . . A
man knows it must be, and submits. It will do him no good to
whine." '[1]

IV

There was a very practical side to Johnson's religion. The
eighteenth century had a passion for sermons. Johnson himself
not only wrote a large number for clerical friends—like Dr
Taylor, the bucolic and simoniacal rector of Market Bosworth—
but had ideas far before his age about ministerial life and work
generally. Witness the *Letter to a Young Clergyman in the Country*[2]
—the Rev. Charles Laurence, son of Dr Laurence, Johnson's
physician and friend, and a direct descendant of Milton's
'Laurence of virtuous father, virtuous son'. This letter, full of
mellow wisdom and the soundest and kindest of common sense
is curiously little known, and I have never seen any reference to
it in any book on Homiletics or Practical Training.

Even better than Johnson's precept in religious matters was
his example. Never a wealthy man, though the pension of
£300 a year which Lord Bute, much to his credit, secured for
him from the Royal Bounty[3]—made him financially independent for the rest of his life, Johnson was little short of reckless
in secret charities to those who could not possibly repay him,
and were, more often than not, unworthy and ungrateful. His
friends' remonstrances could not shake him. 'Johnson had a
natural imbecility about him', said the *unclubable* Hawkins,
'arising from humanity and pity to the sufferings of his fellow-
creatures, that was prejudicial to his interests'; and Mrs
Thrale, with one of those genuine flashes of insight which
redeem so much of her flightiness and intellectual snobbery,

[1] Boswell's *Life*, October, 1769.
[2] Given in full in Boswell's *Life*, 30 August 1780.
[3] Despite Johnson's well-known anti-Hanoverian sympathies and the
famous definition of *pension* in the *Dictionary:* 'An allowance made to any one.
without an equivalent. In England it is generally understood to mean pay
given to a state hireling for treason to his country.'

adds her testimony: 'Concerning the poor, he really loved them as nobody else does—with a desire they should be happy.'

Mrs Thrale's long and close friendship with Johnson completely destroyed any illusions she may have had about him in the early prime of her lion-hunting days. Some of her passing remarks bring him very near to us. 'The coldest and most languid hearers of the word must have felt themselves animated by his manner of reading the Holy Scriptures, and to pray by his sick-bed required strength of body as well of mind, so vehement were his manners, and his tones of voice so pathetic.' Again: 'In answer to the arguments used by Puritans, Quakers, etc., against showy decorations of the human figure, I once heard him exclaim, "Oh let us not be found when our Master calls us, ripping the lace off our waistcoats, but the spirit of contention from our souls and tongues! Let us all conform in outward customs, which are of no consequence, to the manners of those whom we live among, and despise such paltry distinctions. Alas (continued he) a man who cannot get to heaven in a green coat, will not find his way thither the sooner in a grey one." '

If we wish to know what Streatham Park meant to Johnson, it is not so much to Mrs Thrale's *Diaries*, still less to the Autolycus-like 'snappers up of unconsidered trifles' in our own days, that we must turn, but rather to Johnson's altogether charming letters to 'Queenie' Thrale, and that most touching farewell to what had been a home to him for more than sixteen years.

'October 6th, 1782. Almighty God, Father of all mercy, help me, by Thy grace, that I may with humble and sincere thankfulness remember the comforts and conveniences which I have enjoyed at this place, and that I may resign them with holy submission, equally trusting in Thy protection, when Thou givest, and when Thou takest away. Have mercy upon me, O Lord, have mercy upon me. To thy fatherly protection, O Lord, I commend this family. Bless, guide, and defend them, that they may so pass through this world as finally to enjoy in Thy presence everlasting happiness, for Jesus Christ's sake.

Amen . . . October 7. I was called early. I packed up my bun-
dles, and used the foregoing Prayer with my morning devotions, somewhat I think, enlarged. Being earlier than the family, I read St Paul's farewell in the Acts, and then fortuitously
in the Gospels, which was my parting use of the library.'[1]

V

Johnson lived for two years more—years of which Carlyle
wrote very beautifully:

'If Destiny had beaten hard on poor Samuel, and did never
cease to visit him too roughly, yet the last section of his Life
might be pronounced victorious and on the whole happy . . .
Early friends had long sunk into the grave; yet in his soul they
ever lived, fresh and clear, with soft pious breathings towards
them, not without a still hope of one day meeting them again
in purer union. Such was Johnson's Life: the victorious Battle
of a free, true Man. Finally he died the death of the free and
true; a dark cloud of Death, solemn, and not untinged with
haloes of immortal Hope 'took him away', and our eyes could
no longer behold him; but can still behold the trace and impress of his courageous, honest spirit, deep-legible in the World's
Business, wheresoever he walked and was.'[2]

This is true in the main, but somewhat idyllic in expression.
The general impression one gathers from the closing pages of
Boswell is rather that of an old man with a new gentleness and
considerateness, very touching in one formerly so formidable,
but with health much broken, the old fear of death still haunting him many an hour by day and night.

One remembers his saying to Boswell fifteen years before
(19 October 1769), 'meditating upon the awful hour of his
own dissolution, and in what manner he should conduct himself upon that occasion: "I know not, whether I should wish
to have a friend by me, or have it all between God and myself."' Happily, he never needed to make the choice. With
unselfish loyalty and devotion friends gathered round the old
man's sickbed, glad to do what they could in cheering him on

[1] *Prayers and Meditations*, p. 211.
[2] *Essay on Johnson*.

what they and he knew must be the last journey. His physicians
were unwearied in their care, and refused to take a farthing
for their services. Burke, Langton, Reynolds, Windham, Hawkins, all gave up many hours in their busy lives in order to sit
by his bedside. One friend alone was absent, detained in
Scotland, to his own sorrow, and to the lasting loss of every
reader of his book.

What Boswell did in bringing his great task to a close, was
to take the day-to-day memoranda which Hoole and Hawkins
and others had already set down, to cross-question the various
witnesses on certain points of detail, and to weave together all
this miscellaneous material into as connected a narrative as
possible. He succeeded wonderfully, but, notwithstanding all
his efforts, his touch for once is curiously uncertain. There
are gaps, overlappings, redundancies, and comparatively little
of that vividness and intimacy which in many a page of the
Life make us free of the finest company in the world. Once
and again one is conscious of a certain *stammer*, as though the
writer were uneasy and could not bring himself to say what
his literary conscience would not allow him to suppress. He
has told us that, amid all Johnson's sufferings in his last illness,
the gentleness which had surprised many who had known him
well, now became more marked than ever, and that, for several
days before the end the old spectres of fear and gloom were
altogether and finally exorcised. As Macaulay puts it in his
biography of Johnson,[1] written for the *Encyclopaedia Britannica*
—'a piece of English literature of the very first order', as
Matthew Arnold well styles it—'His temper became unusually
patient and gentle: he ceased to think with terror of death
and of that which lies beyond death, and he spoke much of
the mercy of God and of the propitiation of Christ. In this
serene frame of mind he died.'

[1] This biography written for the eighth Edition of the *Encyclopaedia* appears unaltered in the ninth Edition. In the eleventh and subsequent
editions it appears as revised by Thomas Seccombe, who says in an explana-
tory note, 'Macaulay's text has been retained with a few trifling modifica-
tions in which his invincible love of the picturesque has drawn him de-
monstrably aside from the dull line of verity.' What those 'trifling modi-

Was there anything to account for such a noticeable change in Johnson, and also to explain that curious *stammer* in the narrative, Boswell's anxious disclaimer of 'fanaticism', one significant suppression by Dr Strahan, and the peevish surprise of Sir John Hawkins that a High Churchman like Johnson 'should be driven to seek for spiritual comfort in the writings of sectaries'? I think there is such evidence.

In Hannah More's *Memoirs*[1] may be read a very interesting letter, which, according to the editor, the Rev. Mr Roberts, was found among her papers after her death. This letter from the Rev. J. Sanger to Lady Lifford, a well-known Irish Evangelical, runs as follows:

'Dr Johnson had expressed great dissatisfaction with himself on the approach of death . . . and was not to be comforted by the ordinary topics of consolation which were addressed to him. In consequence, he desired to see a clergyman, and particularly described the views and character of the person whom he wished to consult. After some consideration, a Mr Winstanley was named.[2] The Doctor requested Sir John Hawkins to write a note in his name, requesting Mr Winstanley's attendance as a minister.[3] Mr Winstanley, who was in a very weak state of health, was quite overpowered on receiving this note, and felt appalled by the very thought of encountering the talents and learning of Dr Johnson. In his embarrassment he went to his friend Colonel Pownall, . . . asking him for his advice how to

---

fications' are, may be learned from a comparison of the two versions. With much else, the sentences quoted above have been expunged. Macaulay, it must be remembered, not only knew his Boswell and the abundant relevant literature by heart, but, as a writer in *Macmillan's Magazine*, February 1860, on 'Macaulay as a Boy' says, 'Through Hannah More as through a secondary memory, he had a more vivid tradition of the English literary society of the Eighteenth Century, and of the personal habits of Johnson and his contemporaries, than might otherwise have been possible.'

One feels that a protest against such drastic and tendentious 'editorship' is necessary.

[1] Vol. I, p. 377.
[2] This was the Rector of St Dunstan's-in-the-East, who, some three or four years before this date, had proved himself a very good friend to George Crabbe the poet in the hour of his direst need.
[3] Hawkins in his *Life of Johnson* makes no mention of this.

act. The Colonel, who was a pious man, urged him immediately to follow what appeared to be a remarkable leading of Providence, and for a time argued his friend out of his nervous
apprehension. But after he had left Colonel Pownall, Mr Winstanley's fears returned in so great a degree as to prevail upon
him to abandon the thought of a personal interview with the
Doctor. He determined in consequence to write him a letter.

' "Sir, I beg to acknowledge the honour of your note, and am
very sorry that the state of my health prevents my compliance
with your request: but my nerves are so shattered that I feel
as if I should be quite confounded by your presence, and, instead of promoting, should only injure, the cause in which you
desire my aid. Permit me therefore to write what I would wish
to say, were I present. I can easily conceive what would be the
subjects of your inquiry. . . On whichever side you look, you
see only positive transgressions or defective obedience; and
hence, in self-despair are eagerly inquiring, "What shall I do
to be saved?" I say to you in the language of the Baptist, "Behold the Lamb of God which taketh away the sin of the
world." ' . . . When Sir John Hawkins came to this part of Mr
Winstanley's letter, the Doctor interrupted him, anxiously asking, "Does he say so? Read it again, Sir John." Sir John complied: upon which the Doctor said, "I must see that man; write
again to him." A second note was accordingly sent; but even
this repeated solicitation could not prevail over Mr Winstanley's fears. He was led, however, by it to write again to the Doctor, renewing and enlarging upon the subject of his first letter,
and these communications, together with the conversation of
the late Mr Latrobe who was a particular friend of Dr Johnson,
appeared to have been blessed by God in bringing this great
man to the renunciation of self, and a simple reliance on Jesus
as his Saviour.'

This seems to me, despite all its old-fashioned, pietistic
phraseology, a very straightforward narrative, none the less
credible because Mr Winstanley plays a somewhat unheroic
part in the whole business. At the same time, I think we can
understand why there should have been a certain hesitation
about the expediency of its publication by any one in Johnson's immediate circle. Feeling ran high in those days between
Evangelical and High Church. We can gather from allusions

in Wilberforce's Letters and elsewhere that there was a
definite amount of floating tradition about Johnson's 'conversion'. John Wilson Croker—perhaps the most detested man of
his time, of whom it was once said, that he 'would go a hundred miles through sleet and snow, in a December night, to
search a parish register, for the sake of showing that a man
was illegitimate, or a woman older than she said she was'[1]—
made certain investigations after the publication of the narrative, attempting to shake its credibility. It may be conceded
that the 'Rigby' of *Coningsby*, the 'Wenham' of *Pendennis*, was
not the kind of person most fit to judge of the evidence in such
a case.

In a notice of Hannah More's *Memoirs* in *The Quarterly
Review* for November 1834, written, if one may judge from the
style, by John Gibson Lockhart, at that time editor, a flood of
invective is let loose on the 'indiscreetness in which authors of
his class'—this refers to the editor of the *Memoirs*, Mr Roberts
—'are apt to indulge when they see or fancy the slightest
opportunity of insinuating anything to the disparagement of
the rational and immense majority of the religious public in
this country—their faith and practice'; and then goes on:

'Mr Croker's annihilation . . . of the romance about Mr Latrobe is complete and perfect: and as to the story of Mr Winstanley, it is enough to say that no such person is named, either
by *Sir John Hawkins*, or in *any other* of the accounts of Johnson's
life hitherto published. The whole of this circumstantial narrative is therefore a dream, a blunder, or more probably a bung-
ling piece of quackery,—a pious fraud. In any view, this attempt to persuade us that Dr Johnson's mind was not made
up as to the great fundamental doctrine of the Christian religion until it was enforced on him *in extremis* by sectarian or
Methodistical zeal, cannot redound to the credit of Mr
Roberts' understanding. . . But enough of Dr Johnson.'

And enough of the *Quarterly Reviewer* and his pontifical asser-
tions. At the same time, it is rather curious to read Lockhart's
scornful denunciation of the very offence for which he was
himself to be charged—I cannot but think on insufficient

[1] *The Maclise Portrait Gallery*, ed. Bates, p. 73.
c

evidence—in connection with his own famous account of the last days of Sir Walter Scott.

It is good to leave the regions of controversy, and to read the Prayer which Johnson wrote for the Communion Service held in his room, little more than a week before his death:

'Almighty and most merciful Father, I am now as to human eyes it seems about to commemorate for the last time the death of Thy Son Jesus Christ our Saviour and Redeemer. Grant, O Lord, that my whole hope and confidence may be in His merits, and in Thy mercy. Forgive and accept my late conversion; enforce and accept my imperfect repentance; make this communion available to the confirmation of my faith, the establishment of my hope, and the enlargement of my charity, and make the death of Thy Son Jesus effectual to my redemption. Have mercy upon me, and pardon the multitude of my offences. Bless my friends, have mercy upon all men. Support me by the grace of Thy Holy Spirit in the days of weakness and at the hour of death; and receive me, at my death, to everlasting happiness, for the sake of Jesus Christ. Amen.'[1]

'He joined', we are told, 'in every part of the service, and in this prayer, with great fervour of devotion,' and thereafter, ' "I have taken my viaticum. I hope I shall arrive safe at the end of my journey, and be accepted at last." ' Next day he made his will, prefixing it, on the suggestion of Hawkins, with 'such an explicit declaration of his belief as might obviate all suspicions that he was any other than a Christian'. ' "I humbly commit to the infinite and eternal goodness of Almighty God, my soul polluted with many sins; but, as I hope, purified by repentance, and redeemed, as I trust, by the death of Jesus Christ." '[2] Despite great exhaustion and severe spasms of pain, he refused

---

[1] The above is an exact copy of Johnson's autograph MS., now in possession of Professor C. B. Tinker. In *Prayers and Meditations*—both the MS. of the prayer in Dr Strahan's (the Editor's) handwriting and the official printed copy—the clause 'Forgive and accept my late conversion' is expunged. See Note in G. Birkbeck Hill's Edition of Boswell's *Life*, Revised Edition, Vol. IV, Appendix J, p. 553.

[2] Hawkins in *Johnsonian Miscellanies*, Vol. II, p. 125. The version of Boswell's *Life* is much shorter: 'I bequeath to God, a soul polluted by many sins, but I hope purified by JESUS CHRIST.'

to take any opiates, 'for', said he, 'I have prayed that I may
render up my soul to God unclouded.' So, about seven o'clock
in the evening of Monday, 13 December 1784, he passed

Ex umbris et imaginibus in veritatem.

VI

It would be hard to overestimate the influence, direct and
indirect, which Johnson exercised on the whole attitude of his
contemporaries towards religion. Deeply read in the older
works of divinity as he was, and always setting his powerful
faculties to play freely on the greatest of themes—God, the
World, the Soul—Johnson was never, in the strict sense, an
original thinker. He had the typical English dislike for, and
distrust of, speculation *in vacuo*. All his thinking, like that of
Søren Kierkegaard, was deeply tinged by the hardships, at
times the horrors, of his own experience. But if we consider
the influence of those beliefs

> On that best portion of a good man's life,
> His little, nameless, unremembered acts
> Of kindness and of love,

we find ourselves in a different world. The stricter Evangelicals
of that time looked with a certain suspicion on Johnson's intimate association with men and women who were frankly
worldly, many of them free-thinkers, some of them loose livers.
They lamented that such brilliant powers as his, instead of
concentrating on what they considered some distinctively
Christian work, should expend themselves in ephemeral talk.
But Carlyle has well emphasized the impressiveness of the fact
that, in such an age, a man of Johnson's stature should whole-
heartedly identify himself with Christian faith and Christian
standards. In Mrs Thrale's salon, at the weekly meeting of
The Club or other gathering of the 'Wits', or at a dinner-party
at Dilly's, he was always the central figure; and, as Sir Joshua
Reynolds said, 'he would never suffer the least immorality or
indecency of conversation to proceed without a severe check'.
In the presence of such a champion of the Faith, open scoffers

like Wilkes and Foote were constrained to 'keep their mouths with a bridle'. And all who cared might see him in his pew in the north gallery of St Clement Danes Church—now, alas, smashed to pieces by enemy action in the Battle of London—or humbly kneeling at the altar-rails some Easter Sunday, side by side with 'a poor girl at the Sacrament in a bedgown, to whom I gave privately a crown, though I saw Hart's *Hymns* in her hand'.

There was no figure better known in London streets from Temple Bar to the Royal Exchange; and merely to know that Johnson was there, holding his own and far more than his own against all comers, was, to hundreds of plain Christian folk, something like the sight of the White Plume at the Battle of Ivry to the soldiers of Henry of Navarre.

Some also knew him in quite a different character, as a man, with all his formidableness, not at all unlike that troublesome *Mr Fearing* in *The Pilgrim's Progress*, who, after he had started on his journey, 'lay roaring at the *Slough of Dispond*, for above a month together. *He would not go back again neither. . .* He had, I think, a *Slough of Dispond* in his Mind, a *Slough* that he carried everywhere with him. . . When we came at the Hill *Difficulty* he made no stick at that, nor did he much fear the Lions: For you must know that his Trouble *was not about such things as those*, his Fear was about his Acceptance at last'. Like *Mr Fearing*, too, 'he always loved good talk . . . and when he was come at *Vanity Fair*, he would have fought with all the men in the Fair . . . so hot was he against their Fooleries. . . But when he was come at the *River* where was no Bridge, there again he was in a heavy case; now, now he said he should be drowned for ever, and so never see that Face with Comfort, that he had come so many miles to behold. And here also I took notice of what was very remarkable, the Water of that River was lower at this time than ever I saw it in all my Life: so he went over at last, not much above wet-shod.'

Mrs Thrale tells that in repeating the *Dies Irae*, Johnson never could pass one particular stanza without bursting into a flood of tears. The words of that stanza were at the very roots of his religion, and reveal the secret of his life. They are the

most moving words in the whole range of the literature of
devotion:

> QUAERENS ME, SEDISTI LASSUS:
> REDEMISTI, CRUCEM PASSUS:
> TANTUS LABOR NON SIT CASSUS!

JOHN NEWTON

A VINDICATION

IN the very heart of the City of London, at the sharp angle where Lombard Street meets King William Street, and within a stone's throw of the Bank, the Royal Exchange, and the Mansion House, stands a famous City church, St Mary Woolnoth, built by Nicholas Hawkesmoor, one of Sir Christopher Wren's pupils, in the reign of George the First. Within the quaint, square Georgian interior, with its twelve beautiful fluted Corinthian columns and mahogany pulpit, and the banners of the Goldsmiths' Company hanging from the west gallery, the roar of London at midday, only a few yards distant, sounds as faint and far away as the murmur of the sea in a shell. On the north wall, close by the vestry door, is a marble tablet with an inscription which gives the church its chief interest:

'John Newton||Clerk||once an infidel and libertine||a servant of slaves in Africa||was||by the rich mercy||of our Lord and Saviour||Jesus Christ, preserved, restored, pardoned||and|| appointed to preach the faith||he had long laboured to destroy.|| He ministered||near xvi years as Curate and Vicar||of Olney in Bucks||and xxviii years as Rector||of these United Parishes||On Feb the first MDCCL he married||Mary||daughter of the late George Catlett||of Chatham, Kent||whom he resigned||to the Lord who gave her||on Dec. the xv, MDCCXC.'

That, with the exception of the dates of his own birth and death, is a succinct account of the life of John Newton, and even were there no other biographical material, it would make it plain that the writer—for Newton himself left strict injunctions that no other monument or inscription should be attempted—was no common man.

But there is an almost embarrassing wealth of material. From comparatively early in life to extreme old age—he died at eighty-two—Newton was continually writing. His complete works—sermons, treatises, autobiographies in various recensions, verses, letters without end—have been collected into a

24

massive volume of considerably over a thousand double-columned pages. Few would care to make an attempt upon it nowadays, and much of it has long been dead. Yet one can hardly open the book anywhere and read a few sentences without coming on something robust and racy, alike in thought and expression. One particular autobiographical fragment is as vivid and realistic as anything in Defoe or Marryat. Of *Letters to a Wife: written during three voyages to Africa* no less distinguished a critic than Edward FitzGerald said, 'It contains some of the most beautiful things I ever read: fine feeling in fine English'; and it is safe to say that some of the verses, though found in no anthology of English verse, will, by virtue of a certain stark and unselfconscious simplicity and directness, live as long as the language.

Moreover, both in his lifetime and even more since his death, people have taken sides about Newton, and to this day there are writers who cannot even mention his name without quite evidently losing their temper and indulging in violent and abusive expressions, most of all in connection with his relations to one who for many years was his most intimate friend, William Cowper.

Newton was pre-eminently a man of his time: of what Matthew Arnold once called 'our age of prose and reason, our excellent and indispensable Eighteenth Century.'[1] The gown and bands and bushy white wig, and the sturdy commonsense aspect of the man, somewhat marred by a squint like Edward Irving's, in the portrait facing the title-page of the *Collected Works*, place and date him as unmistakably as Reynolds's famous portrait places Dr Johnson. I have not come across any record of an actual meeting of the two men, though for five years each lived within a mile of the other, and few figures could have been more familiar in London streets than Samuel Johnson and John Newton.

Newton was born in London—parish or district not specified —on the 24 July 1725. His father was for many years a shipmaster in the Mediterranean trade. Later in life he joined the Hudson Bay Company's service, and became Governor of

[1] *Introduction to Ward's English Poets.*

York Fort—that dreary outpost in the North Western Wilderness which all readers of R. M. Ballantyne's *The Young Fur Traders* will remember. There he was drowned while bathing in 1751, shortly after his son's *sturm und drang* period in Africa was over. His mother was a very good woman, who gave her boy his earliest lessons, storing his memory with passages of Scripture, teaching him the Shorter Catechism with the proofs, and Watts's *Divine and Moral Songs for Children*; making a beginning also with Latin; all before he was six years old! But he throve on this strong fare, and as he says, 'seemed as willing to learn as my mother was to teach me'. It was her ambition that her only child should become a minister, and she had planned to send him to study at St Andrews; but she died of consumption before he was seven. Newton never forgot her or the lessons she taught him, all through the wild years and devious wanderings that were so soon to follow.

His father, who had been at sea when his wife died, soon married again, and, presumably to give the boy a taste for his own profession, took him away from school when he was eleven years old, to be with him on his own ship. The next six years were spent mostly in voyaging up and down the Mediterranean, and in long stays in one or other of the ports—worst of all schools for a growing lad. The little schooling he had got before he went to sea was soon forgotten, but the boy's eager, inquiring mind and restless disposition led him into all sorts of strange places. Sometimes he tried to live by strict rule, but ever and again broke away from all restraint. His father was a just man, but stern and distant in manner, and the boy was heartily afraid of him. 'I am persuaded he loved me, but he seemed not willing that I should know it.' But when Newton was seventeen, on a visit to distant relatives in Kent, he met his future wife, Mary Catlett, then a schoolgirl of thirteen.

'I soon lost all sense of religion, and became deaf to the remonstrances of conscience and prudence: but my regard for her was always the same: and I may perhaps venture to say that none of the scenes of misery and wickedness I afterwards experienced, ever banished her a single hour together from my waking thoughts for the seven following years.'

Chequered years these were for him. On a Dutch bookstall
he had picked up a stray volume of Shaftesbury's *Characteristics*,
and, fascinated by the style in which it was written, soon had
the book by heart. The reading of other sceptical books followed, and having been thrown into very rough company—for
in disobedience to his father who had procured him an opening
in Jamaica as a planter, he had shipped as a common seaman
on board a Mediterranean trader—he became more and more
lax in conduct. On his return to England in 1743, having been
imprudent enough to go about in a seaman's checked shirt, he
was seized by a press-gang and haled on board a man-of-war.
It was the year of Dettingen, and French fleets were patrolling
the Channel. His father could not procure his release, but he
made interest with the Captain of the ship who, struck with
the lad's capacity, gave him a midshipman's berth. Having a
day on shore, however, Newton made off for Kent to see Mary
Catlett, and then, realizing that he had outstayed his leave,
deserted. When caught he was taken through the streets of
Plymouth by an armed guard, degraded from his rank, put in
irons, and publicly flogged.

'My breast was filled with the most excruciating passions,
eager desire, bitter rage, and black despair . . . I cannot express with what wishfulness and regret I cast my last looks upon
the English shore, . . . and when I could see it no longer, I
was tempted to throw myself into the sea. . . But the secret
hand of God restrained me. . . Though I had well deserved all
I met with, and the Captain might have been justified if he
had carried his resentment still further, yet my pride at that
time suggested that I had been grossly injured: and this so far
wrought upon my wicked heart, that I actually formed designs
against his life; and this was one reason that made me willing
to prolong my own. . . I had not the least fear of God before
my eyes, nor (so far as I remember) the least sensibility of conscience. But when I had chosen death rather than life, a ray of
hope would come in . . . that I should yet see better days: that
I might again return to England, and have my wishes crowned
if I did not wilfully throw myself away. In a word, my love to
Mary Catlett was now the only restraint I had left. Though I
neither feared God nor regarded men, I could not bear that

she should think meanly of me when I was dead... This single thought which had not restrained me from a thousand smalle evils, proved my only and effectual barrier against the greatest and most fatal temptations.'

The fleet was bound for the East Indies, and as the voyage in those days was round the Cape of Good Hope, it might last anything from six to nine months. Newton was determined that he would not go to India, and that, by hook or by crook, he would find his way to Guinea. It would appear that even thus early in life there was something dominating and formidable in his personality. We can well believe that the captain would be thankful enough to get quit of such a sullen and dangerous young fellow, who had begun to show, in addition to other gifts, a power of writing ribald and mutinous songs, which he taught to the ship's company. Little wonder that Newton got his wish, and was transferred at Madeira to a ship in the Guinea Coasting trade, and that H.M.S. *Harwich* sailed away on its long voyage south and east, thankful, like Dogberry, to be 'rid of a knave'.

Now begins that episode in Newton's life that every one associates with him: his nine years' connection with slaves and the slave-trade. Up till then, the trade from the Guinea Coast to the West Indies was considered, if not a desirable, yet a legitimate, way of making a living. More than forty years were to elapse before Clarkson and Granville Sharp formed the Society for the Suppression of the Slave Trade, and Newton himself was to write his manly and pathetic *Thoughts upon the African Slave Trade*:

'If my testimony should not be necessary or serviceable, yet perhaps I am bound in conscience to take shame to myself by a public confession, which, however sincere, comes too late to prevent or repair the misery and mischief to which I have formerly been accessory.'

Dr Johnson, in the way in which he regarded the slave-trade as in many other matters, was ahead of his time, but Boswell, while transcribing his arguments against slavery, at once records his own dissent and protest.

'To abolish a *status* which in all ages God has sanctioned and
man has continued, would not only be *robbery* to an innumer-
able class of our fellow-subjects: but it would be extreme cruelty to the African savages, a portion of whom it saves from
massacre or intolerable bondage in their own country, and
introduces into a much happier state of life; especially now
when their passage to the West Indies and their treatment
there is humanely regulated. To abolish this trade would be
to . . . shut the gates of mercy on mankind.'[1]

On board the coasting vessel in which he now found himself
Newton was among strangers, and any restraint that he had
had perforce to exercise hitherto, he now cast off. It was a
hard-drinking age, yet he seems never to have given way to
that vice. But, as he confesses, there was no other depth of
active wickedness to which he did not sink; he even became a
master in the blackest sin of all, the leading of others to become
worse than himself.

So dangerous was he, that the mate of the ship was glad to
let him go on land, and become the servant of a slave-trader
who lived on the Plaintain Islands, some sixty miles to the
south of Sierra Leone. It was the darkest hour of Newton's life.
Even the negroes thought themselves too good to speak to him.
One black woman, the mistress of the trader, took all the
delight of a petty and vindictive nature in ill-treating and
insulting him in every possible way, hounding on the slaves in
the absence of his master against the prodigal who was now
experiencing a worse fate than herding swine or eating husks.
Despised, rejected, starved, till he was glad to eat raw roots
from the plantations, burned up with fever, with hardly even
rags to cover his body from the incessant rain, the poor lad—
he was only nineteen—yet showed the mental energy that
nothing could tame. The one book he had with him was a

---

[1] *Life of Johnson*, p. 433. Similarly Nelson wrote from the *Victory:* 'I was
bred in the good old school, and taught to appreciate the value of our West
Indian possessions, and neither in the field nor in the Senate shall their just
rights be infringed, while I have an arm to fight in their defence, or a tongue
to launch my voice against the damnable doctrine of Wilberforce and his
hypocritical allies.' Quoted in *Life of Zachary Macaulay*, by Lady Knutsford,
p. 258.

Euclid, and with this he would betake himself to a remote corner of the island by the seaside, and draw diagrams with a long stick upon the sand. 'Thus [he says] I often beguiled my sorrows, and almost forgot my feeling.'[1]

After a time—being little better than a slave himself, and certainly less humanely treated—he was transferred to another master with whom his lot was easier. But, living among the natives, themselves further degraded by contact with outcast Europeans, he became what was significantly termed on that coast 'a white man grown black'.

In his former wretchedness he had written to his father, who at once sent orders for a search to be made for him at Sierra Leone. But no trace of him could be found, and it was only after a series of extraordinary providences that he was discovered and, after two years of this castaway life, put on board a ship trading up and down the Oil Rivers and the Gold and Ivory Coasts. Here again his seemingly irreclaimable wildness

---

[1] Dr John W. Oliver, Edinburgh, hearing the writer quote this passage from the *Narrative*, drew his attention to the following passage in Wordsworth's *Prelude* (Book vi, p. 272):

> 'Tis told by one whom stormy waters threw,
> With fellow-sufferers by the shipwreck spared,
> Upon a desert-coast, that having brought
> To land a single volume, saved by chance,
> A treatise of Geometry, he wont,
> Although of food and clothing destitute,
> And beyond common wretchedness depressed,
> To part from company and take this book
> (Then first a self-taught pupil in its truths)
> To spots remote, and draw his diagrams
> With a long staff upon the sand, and thus
> Did oft beguile his sorrow, and almost
> Forget his feeling . . .

Professor de Selincourt, in his monumental edition of *The Prelude*, made no reference to this parallel. Subsequently, however, he stated that he had come across the Newton passage in one of Dorothy Wordsworth's early note-books devoted to transcripts of her brother's poems. The writing being bad, he misread the name of Newton as Nelson, and so the clue was missed. Professor Havens noted the Newton source in his *The Mind of a Poet*, his exhaustive commentary on *The Prelude*.

broke out. His blasphemies shocked even the hardened sailors who, when storms broke on the ship, looked on him as a Jonah. 'I seemed to have every mark of final impenitence and rejection; neither judgements nor mercies made the least impression on me.' Yet now and again compunction visited him.

The ship had crossed to Brazil, then held straight northward from the banks of Newfoundland on its homeward voyage. It was badly out of gear, and the spring equinoctial gales were blowing hard. Little could be done in navigating the vessel, and, to pass the time, Newton picked up one of the very few books which chanced to be on board. Of all the books in the world this was Thomas à Kempis, and as he read the quiet, beautiful sentences of the old cloistered saint, the thought came into his mind, 'What if these things should be true?' He shut the book hastily, climbed into his hammock, and fell fast asleep. 'But now', as he says, 'the Lord's time was come.' On the morning of the 10 March 1748 he was awakened by the sound of heavy seas breaking on the deck. A fearful tempest had fallen on the ship, and for four days it raged with uninterrupted fury. The vessel was waterlogged, and became partly a wreck, and several of the crew were washed overboard. Newton himself was lashed to the pumps, and toiled like a giant for hours together as the vessel drifted helplessly eastward. All hope was abandoned. Then, as he tells the story, old, half-forgotten, often-derided words of the Bible came to his memory, especially words of judgement. Scene after scene of his recent life rose up before him. The storm lulled somewhat, and then he began to pray. 'My prayer was like the cry of the ravens, which yet the Lord does not disdain to hear.'

I cannot follow out the whole story in detail as Newton tells it: how the storm broke out again; how they hailed what they supposed to be the coast of Ireland, only to find it was but a bank of fog; how they drifted about to the west of the Hebrides, and finally, four weeks after they had been struck by the storm, crept to land in Lough Swilly on the coast of Ulster, more dead than alive, and with provisions practically gone.

This was the turning-point of Newton's life. Henceforth he never failed to keep the 10 March in solemn remembrance

and thanksgiving. From that time his face was set towards the
light, though it did not shine fully upon him for many a day.

He had proved his capacity in seamanship, and henceforward was no longer before the mast. He had written his father
begging his forgiveness, but though he received one or two kind
letters in return, he was too late to see him; for he had left for
Hudson Bay, whence ere long the news came of his death.
Before leaving England, however, the father had withdrawn
the objections he had imposed—little wonder!—on his son's
engagement to Mary Catlett. Her friends also, seeing a change
in the young man, were willing, and when Newton once more
sailed for Africa, it was agreed that the marriage should take
place as soon as he should have obtained command of a ship.
He could have got this almost at once, but wisely preferred
first to gain what experience he could as mate.

His seaman's duties were not enough to occupy his energies,
and he resolved to take up again the Latin that his mother had
begun to teach him when he was a child. He had no dictionary,
but set to work to spell his way through a Delphin Horace,
with the aid of a Latin Bible and an English translation which
he had picked up. It might seem an almost incredible feat; and
there is something almost grotesque in the thought of reading
Horace by the help of the Vulgate! But the feat was achieved,
and from that day onward he had Horace practically by heart.
In later voyages he remembered to take a dictionary, and read
through Juvenal, Livy, Sallust, Caesar, Virgil, and Terence.
Later, he picked up enough Hebrew and Greek to read the
Bible in the original. Strangely enough, he tells us that he
never read any of the Greek classics. But he became more and
more a student of the Bible, and the desire began to rise within
him—perhaps from some hazy recollections of childhood and
his mother's wishes—that he might yet become a minister.

As yet, he had no prospect of any livelihood but the sea and
the Guinea trade. However, being now promised the command
of a ship, he came home, and was married to Mary Catlett on
12 February 1750. Their marriage lasted for almost forty-one
years, and was a romance from first to last. After six months
at home, he set out on the second of his voyages to the Guinea

coast. Of course his wife could not accompany him to a climate
so deadly to Europeans, and so began that series of *Letters to a
Wife* of which Edward FitzGerald thought so highly. Newton's
habit was to write daily, and, at every port where there was a
chance of falling in with a ship sailing for England, to send
home a large packet. He tells, too, of a custom they had both
agreed upon, of looking at the Pole-star at a certain hour
every evening when the sky was clear. All through the series
of letters—there are more than fifty pages of them, short and
long, written in sickness and health at all sorts of times and
places, up the steaming tropical rivers and amid the man-
grove swamps, and out on the high seas—he pours out his
thoughts and feelings with entire unreserve. He writes with a
curious unconcern of his employment as captain of a slaver
with a full cargo of human chattels on board, bound from
Africa to the West Indian plantations. In a note to one of the
letters when they appeared in published form, he says:

'The reader may perhaps wonder, as I now myself, that
knowing the state of the vile traffic to be as I have here described, and abounding with enormities which I have not mentioned, I did not at the time start with horror at my own employment as an agent in promoting it. Custom, example, and
interest had blinded my eyes. I did it ignorantly; for I am sure,
had I thought of the slave-trade then as I have thought of it
since, no considerations would have induced me to continue in
it. . . I felt the disagreeableness of the business very strongly.
The office of a gaoler and the restraints under which I was
forced to keep my prisoners were not suitable to my feelings: but I
considered it as the line of life which God in His providence
had allotted me, and as a cross which I ought to bear with
patience and thankfulness till He should be pleased to deliver
me from it. Till then, I only thought myself bound to treat the
slaves under my care with gentleness, and to consult their ease
and convenience as far as was consistent with the safety of the
whole family of whites and blacks on board my ship.'

I have quoted this at length because I think it helps to
explain some words which have often been quoted against
Newton:

'I never knew sweeter or more frequent hours of divine

communion than in my two last voyages to Guinea, when I
was either almost excluded from society on shipboard, or when
on shore amongst the natives.'

Lurid pictures have been drawn of Newton at his devotions,
or even writing hymns in his cabin while the chained slaves
sickened and died below in all the horrors of the Middle Passage, of 'the Lord's Table spread across that slave track', and
the 'conflicting emotions of the same John Newton as arch-
slaver and arch-hymn-writer'; and so on. I suppose that to
some of those charges Newton would at once have pleaded
guilty, but we are not to consider him as a Legree, or a blinded
fanatic like some of the Elizabethan captains to whom the poor
slaves were little more than brutes without a reasonable soul,
perpetually under the curse pronounced upon Ham and his
descendants.

His own religious thinking, as he tells us, was as yet confused. But one day at St Kitts he met in a certain Captain
Clunie, the master of a London ship then in port, 'a man of
experience in the things of God and of a lively communicative
turn'. It was a casual meeting in mixed company, but some
word that had fallen from one or the other induced them to
seek each other out in private. Henceforth for a month the two
were almost inseparable.

'He not only informed my understanding, but his discourse
inflamed my heart. He encouraged me to open my mouth in
social prayer; he taught me the advantage of Christian converse; he put me upon an attempt to make my profession more
public and to venture to speak for God. From him or rather
from the Lord by his means, I received an increase of knowledge: my conceptions became clearer and more evangelical
and I was delivered from a fear which had long troubled me,
the fear of relapsing into my former apostasy. . . With these
newly-acquired advantages I left him, and my passage home-
wards gave me leisure to digest what I had received: I had
much comfort and freedom during those seven weeks, and my
sun was seldom clouded.'

His prayers for another kind of life were answered in an
unlooked-for way by a sudden and alarming illness—seemingly

a kind of apoplectic seizure—while he was preparing at Liverpool to set out for another voyage. He recovered quickly, and
from that day onwards till his death, more than fifty years
afterwards, he hardly knew what illness meant. But his doctors
absolutely forbade any more voyages to the Tropics, and Newton was compelled to make a new beginning in life.

After a time he obtained, at Liverpool, a post in the Customs
which was sufficient for his livelihood; but more and more his
thoughts were turning towards the Christian ministry. When
a man such as he turns right round, the world soon comes to
hear about it, and the ex-slave-captain became well-known in
religious circles. At first he had very little gift of utterance, and
he describes his early failures and humiliations with a kind of
rueful humour.

'My first essay as a preacher was in a Dissenting meeting-
house at Leeds in the year 1758. I do not know that I had a
very overweening opinion of my own abilities. I feared and
trembled abundantly, but I was determined to set off *extem-
pore*. I did so. I opened my discourse with a passable exordium,
divided my subject into four heads, had subdivisions under
each in my mind, and was beginning to think I should do pretty
well. But before I had spoken ten minutes, I was stopped like
Hannibal upon the Alps. My ideas forsook me; darkness and
confusion filled up their place. I stood on a precipice and could
not advance a step forward. I stared at the people, and they at
me. But I remained as silent as Friar Bacon's head, and was
forced to come down *re infecta*. . . This disaster made me con-
clude it would be absolutely impossible for me ever to preach
without book. Accordingly I began to compose sermons at full
length. The next time I was asked to preach, I did not feel
much trepidation. I had my discourse in my pocket and did not
much doubt that I was able to read it. But the moment I began, my eyes were riveted to the book, from a fear which got
hold of me, that, if I looked off, I should not readily find the
line again. Thus with my head hanging down (for I am near-
sighted), and fixed like a statue, I conned over my lesson like a
boy learning to read: but I did not stop till I came to the end.
I think I was rather more out of conceit with myself this time
than the former. I had tried the two extremes to little purpose,

D

and there seemed to me to be no medium between them. I
looked sorrowfully at my sermon-book, and said—

Nec tecum, nec sine te.

I began to think that my views to the ministry were presump-
tuous. I thought at least that if the Lord was pleased to accept
my desire to serve Him, He would not accept my service because I had been so vile a creature: as He accepted David's desire to build His house, but did not employ him because he had
shed blood. And yet, notwithstanding all disappointments and
discouragements, He was pleased at length to admit me to His
vineyard.'

It was the age when anything of the nature of 'enthusiasm'
was anathema in the Church of England: 'The pretending to
extraordinary revelations and gifts of the Holy Ghost is a horrid thing; yes, sir, it is a very horrid thing,' as the great and
good Bishop Butler said to John Wesley in Bristol. 'Sir, you
have no business here. You are not commissioned to preach
in this diocese. Therefore I advise you to go hence.'

A man who has come through such fires as Newton had,
bears the mark of them all his life. He is never quite like other
men, and as a rule finds it difficult to fit himself into the
grooves in which they find it a happiness to work. Many of
his friends—Captain Clunie to whom he owed so much, among
them—were Dissenters, and were eager that Newton should
throw in his lot with them. He had also long and close associations with George Whitefield, and could have succeeded him
in Georgia. But he himself had always wished to take orders in
the Church of England, and his wife's influence was strongly
exercised on that side. All sorts of obstacles were thrown in his
way. The Archbishop of York refused to give him ordination,
evidently having doubts of a man who had had such a chequered past, and who even now was friendly with Dissenters,
yet was willing to give up a stated income of £100 a year—
perhaps worth five or six times as much in present value—in
the Liverpool Customs, for an uncertain curacy of £30 to £40
in the Church of England. Newton tells how he got from the
Archbishop the 'softest refusal imaginable'. Still it *was* a
refusal. But the Bishop of Lincoln had more insight than his

superior, and though at the interview with him Newton felt constrained to differ on certain points of doctrine, this was not at all reckoned against him by that good Father in God. He was ordained deacon and then priest in the Countess of Huntingdon's Connexion, and by the good offices of Dr Haweis[1] with Lord Dartmouth, the great patron of the Evangelicals, he was appointed to the curacy of Olney in North Bucks. He entered on his duties there in the end of May 1764, when he was not quite thirty-nine years of age. Then began fifteen strenuous years.

Olney, as Lord David Cecil describes it, is 'a typical small country town with a long straggling High Street and an avenue down the middle of it, a bow-windowed inn, and a roomy Perpendicular Church. But it lacks the cheerful charm associated with such places; its streets are stagnant but not peaceful'.[2] To-day its trade is boot-making. In the middle of the eighteenth century the people were lace-workers, 'ill-paid, fever-stricken, and for the most part as brutal as they were poor.'[3] The surrounding country—meadow-land, in winter waterlogged, through which the sluggish Ouse pursues its lingering course—has been immortalized by Cowper in *The Task*: 'The Winter's Morning Walk' and 'The Winter Walk at Noon.'

The stipend was only £60 a year. But this was supplemented by John Thornton, the wealthy evangelical merchant, by an annual gift of £200, with the charge: 'Be hospitable, and keep open your house for such as are worthy of entertainment. Help the poor and needy. I will stately allow you £200, and readily send you whenever you have occasion for more.' Newton made full and judicious use of this generosity which freed him and his wife from financial care during all the time of their stay at Olney.

The whole country was feeling the thrill and stir of the Evangelical Revival under the preaching of Wesley and Whitefield, and Newton, as a clergyman of the Established Church in

[1] Composer of the tune *Richmond*.
[2] *The Stricken Deer*, p. 310.
[3] Goldwin Smith, *Cowper*, p. 36.

full sympathy with the movement, threw himself with the utmost zeal into an incessant round of services on Sundays and weekdays. Soon the large church was crowded, and, a year after he came to Olney, a gallery was erected along the north side. Even then 'there seemed to be no more room in the body of the church than before.' 'I have often', he writes, 'been engaged about six hours in speaking at church and at home, yet find myself in good case, little or nothing plagued, but if there was occasion, I could readily go and preach again.'

Sixteen years before Robert Raikes in Gloucester, he started a Sunday School or Children's Church in the 'Great House', a big barrack-looking building on the other side of the street from the Vicarage, evidently feeling that he would make more of the children than of their fathers and mothers. If he told them stories in anything like the same fashion as that in which he wrote of his voyage across the Atlantic, we need not wonder that they flocked to him.

The *Narrative* had circulated for a while in manuscript, but it was now published with a preface by Dr Haweis.

'I have reason to hope that the publication of my letters will give some additional weight to my ministry here. The people stare at me since reading them, and well they may. I am indeed a wonder to many, a wonder to myself, especially I wonder that I wonder no more.'[1]

And now comes the episode in Newton's life about which more has been written and greater feeling displayed than about almost any other incident in literary or religious history: his association with William Cowper. Of this he himself writes:

[1] One secret of his influence may be seen by any one who stands in his study at Olney Vicarage. Over the mantel-piece on a large wooden panel may be read in large letters the two texts: AND THOU SHALT REMEMBER THAT THOU WAST A BONDMAN IN THE LAND OF EGYPT, AND THE LORD THY GOD REDEEMED THEE: THEREFORE I COMMAND THEE THIS THING TO-DAY.—Deuteronomy XV. 15. SINCE THOU WAST PRECIOUS IN MY SIGHT, THOU HAST BEEN HONOURABLE, AND I HAVE LOVED THEE: THEREFORE WILL I GIVE MEN FOR THEE, AND PEOPLE FOR THY LIFE.— Isaiah XLIII. 4.

'The Lord who had brought us together so knit our hearts
and affections that for nearly twelve years we were seldom
separated for twelve hours at a time when we were awake and
at home. The first six I passed in daily admiring and trying to
imitate him; during the second six I walked pensively with
him in the valley of the shadow of death.'

It is well in trying to come to a just conclusion on such a
vexed subject, to take the opinions of the two men most concerned, and to set these over against the strongly-coloured
pictures painted by those who, confessedly, are temperamen-
tally out of sympathy with Newton, and against what they
believe to have been his opinions and methods.

Cowper, we must remember, came to Olney in order to be
near Newton, and the two men, differing so greatly, took from
the first a liking to each other which deepened, as the acquain-
tance became close, into intimacy. The two were very different.
It was a case of the ivy and the oak; and it may be freely
admitted that the sturdy tree—one can hardly wonder, remembering the tempests that had beaten upon it—had a thick and
somewhat gnarled bark, round which the beautiful clinging
plant twined itself closely. Add to this, what has already been
said, that Newton was always a dominating personality—far
more so than he was conscious of himself—whether in his
early seafaring days or in shepherding his often recalcitrant
flock at Olney. All this may be granted. But the tendency in
Cowper's biographers has been to exaggerate the weakness and
sensitiveness that were undoubtedly features of his character,
as on the other hand they exaggerate the toughness of Newton's fibre. We must remember that Cowper could not only
pass pleasant minutes holding skeins of silk and worsted for
Mrs Unwin and Lady Hesketh to wind, or write what some-
one has called 'the most comfortable lines in English poetry':

> Now stir the fire, and close the shutters fast,
> Let fall the curtains, wheel the sofa round,
> And while the bubbling and loud hissing urn
> Throws up a steamy column, and the cups,
> That cheer but not inebriate, wait on each,
> So let us welcome peaceful evening in.

He could also, when the spirit so moved him, write 'The Loss
of the Royal George' with its 'vigour of description and the
force of pathos underlying the bare and truly Greek simplicity
of phrase',[1] and 'Boadicea', not to speak of 'John Gilpin', and
scores of the charming letters. Each of the two men found in
the other what was lacking in himself. Newton knew his own
limitations, and felt that he had no more Cowper's gift of song
than Cowper had Newton's own skill in handling a ship in a
gale. He encouraged him to break off the morbid introspection
in which his long hours of leisure tempted him to indulge, by
setting him to visit the poor in Olney and by enlisting his
interest and co-operation in the preparation of the hymn book
of which I shall speak presently.

It will be well, however, to hear what the head and front of
the accusation against Newton is. First let us take Walter
Bagehot:

[John Newton] 'was one of those men who seem intended to
make excellence disagreeable. He was a converting engine.
The whole of his own enormous vigour of body, the whole
steady intensity of a pushing, impelling, compelling, unoriginal
mind, all the mental or corporeal exertion he could exact from
the weak, or elicit from the strong, were devoted to one sole purpose: the effective impact of the Calvinistic tenets on the
parishioners of Olney. No more dangerous adviser, if this world
had been searched over, could have been found for Cowper.
A natural aptitude for dictation, a steady, strong, compelling
decision, great self-command, and a sharp perception of all
impressible points in the character of others, made the task of
guiding weaker brethren a natural and pleasant pursuit. To
suppose that a shrinking, a wounded and tremulous mind like
that of Cowper, would rise against such bold dogmatism, such
hard volition, such animal nerve, is to fancy that the beaten
slave will dare the lash which his very eyes instinctively fear
and shun. Mr. Newton's great idea was that Cowper ought to
be of some use. It never seems to have occurred to him that
so fragile a mind would be unequal to the burden, that a
bruised reed does often break; or rather, if it *did* occur to him,
he regarded it as a subterranean suggestion, and expected a

---

[1] F. T. Palgrave.

supernatural interference to counteract the events at which it hinted. He kept him occupied with subjects which were too great for him; he kept him away from his natural life; he presented to him views and opinions but too well justifying his deep and dark insanity; he convinced him that he ought to experience emotions which were foreign to his nature; he had nothing to add by way of comfort when told that those emotions did not and could not exist. Cowper seems to have felt this. His second illness commenced with a strong dislike to his spiritual adviser, and it may be doubted if there ever was again the same cordiality between them. Mr Newton, too, as was natural, was vexed at Cowper's calamity. His reputation in "the religious world" was deeply pledged to conducting this most "interesting case" to a favourable termination.

'It was to no purpose that Cowper acquired fame and secular glory in the literary world. This was rather adding gall to bitterness. The unbelievers in evangelical religion would be able to point to one at least, and that the best known, among its proselytes, to whom it had not brought peace—whom it had rather confirmed in wretchedness.'[1]

This certainly leaves nothing to be desired for vigour, and one tastes the relish with which it must have been written.

Take again Sir James Frazer, in his preface to an Edition of Cowper's Letters, reprinted in *The Gorgon's Head*[2]—and I must ask you not to judge that most delightful paper by the following extract :

'Newton, a man of robust constitution and iron nerve, had begun life as a captain of a Liverpool Slaver, a profession which he afterwards exchanged for that of a clergyman of the Church of England. That his piety was deep and sincere, and that he had a disinterested affection for Cowper, cannot be doubted; but it seems equally clear that he was very indiscreet, and that the religious stimulants with which he plied Cowper's sensitive and highly-strung nature had a most pernicious influence and were indeed a main cause of the terrible relapse into insanity which the poet suffered a few years after settling at Olney. Nor was Cowper the only victim of the Rev. John Newton's

[1] *Literary Studies*, pp. 43 ff.
[2] pp. 222-4.

injudicious zeal. The reverend gentleman has left it on record
that his name was 'up about the country for preaching people
mad': he knew near a dozen of his flock, most of them pious,
or, as he phrases it, gracious people, who were disordered
in their minds, and he wondered whether the cause was the
sedentary lives the women led over their lace pillows, or the
crowded little rooms in which they lived. The principal cause,
if we may judge by Cowper's case, was Newton himself. . .
Thus more and more isolated and left to the tender mercies of
the Reverend John Newton, Cowper sank into a profound
melancholy, which the composition of the Olney Hymns, un-
dertaken at Newton's suggestion by the two friends jointly in
1771, was hardly of a sufficiently recreative and exhilarating
character to dispel.'

Again:

'Cowper entreated to be allowed to pass the night at the
Vicarage. The request was granted. He went for a night, and
stayed for more than a year, his terrors making it impossible
to remove him except by force, which Newton was too affectionate a friend to employ. We should have had more sympathy
with Newton in this embarrassing situation, if he had not
drawn the trouble on himself by his injudicious conduct. However, in the trying circumstances he seems to have behaved
well, submitting with patience to the humours and fancies of
the poor sufferer, and refusing to accept any pecuniary re-
muneration for the extraordinary expenses to which he was put
by the presence of two unwanted guests.'

And lastly, of Newton leaving for London:

'Olney survived his departure: the effervescence stirred up
by his fiery ministry subsided, and the percentage of lunacy in
the parish visibly declined.'

Thus far the *advocatus diaboli*.

There are biographers of a certain type who would find any
number of excuses for Newton if he had continued his slave-
dealing, but cannot forgive his repentance and conversion; and
who would almost sing their *Nunc dimittis* to any God they
acknowledge if only they could discover some scandal in
Cowper's life. Walter Bagehot and Sir James Frazer are very
far from being of the Strachey order, but I think it can be said

of both that they have no love of what they think is Calvinism. With them it is as with Voltaire, a case of '*Écrasez l'Infame!*' They construct a deductive argument: Cowper's life was darkened by the delusion that he was reprobate; Newton was a Calvinist; therefore *he* was largely responsible for his poor friend's insanity. But, so far as one can trace Cowper's malady, which began four years before he saw Newton, his conviction that he had committed the unpardonable sin and was outcast from God, took the form that this was due to the fact that God had revealed to him that he must destroy himself and that he refused to do so. As Canon Overton says:

'It would have been well for him, since he always held that he had once been a child of God, if he had applied the Calvinistic doctrine of final perseverance to himself. But he looked upon his own as an entirely exceptional case, quite outside of any theological system whatever. . .   From whatever source Cowper may have derived his sad delusion, he certainly did not derive it, or receive any encouragement in it, from anything which Newton taught him, either from the pulpit or elsewhere.'[1]

As to the charge of the unsuitability of the work which Newton gave Cowper to do in visiting the poor and distributing alms, I think Goldwin Smith in his life of Cowper[2] has said the right word:

'The effect of doing good to others on any mind was sure to be good: and the sight of real suffering was like to banish fancied ills. Cowper in this way gained at all events a practical knowledge of the poor, and learned to do them justice though from a rather too theological point of view.'

It is a harrowing picture which Lord David Cecil draws of Cowper's agonies before engaging in public prayer at the meetings in the Great House:

'With set face he nerved himself to the task. For four or five hours before service began he would sit shaking with nerves. Then . . . he would begin to speak. The first sentences came

[1] Abbey and Overton: *The English Church in the Eighteenth Century*, II, 193.
[2] English Men of Letters, p. 41.

toneless and halting; but he gathered strength as he went on.
. . . The worn sensitive features grew tense with an unearthly
enthusiasm, an uncontrollable emotion began to throb in the
quiet educated voice.'

This—will it be believed?—is simply a picturesque expansion,
in Lytton Strachey vein, of three sentences of Newton's:

'For a time his natural constitutional unwillingness to be
noticed in public kept him in silence. But it was not very long
before the ardency of his love to the Saviour and his desire of
being useful to others broke through every restraint. He frequently felt a difficulty and trepidation in the attempt, but
when he had once begun, all difficulty vanished.'

As to the *Olney Hymns*, I think we may be very glad that
Newton induced Cowper to write. English literature as well as
the treasury of devotion would have been much poorer without 'Hark! my Soul, it is the Lord', 'Sometimes a light sur-
prises', ('this brilliant lyric', as Palgrave calls it), and 'Far from
the world, O Lord, I flee', with its exquisite fourth verse,

> There like the nightingale she pours
>   Her solitary lays:
> Nor asks a witness of her song,
>   Nor thirsts for human praise.

The collection as a whole is somewhat depressing in tone, and
the type of theology is stern. Many of the hymns are poor.
Newton, whenever he saw any rhyme that looked as if it might
suit his purpose, promptly fell upon it like a press-gang without
seeking for a better, and never seems to have cared to revise his
first draft. But at its best there is a wonderful reality and
vigour in his work, and often a lyrical rapture with which few
would have been ready to credit him. Witness 'How sweet the
name of Jesus sounds', 'One there is above all others', 'Glorious
things of thee are spoken', 'Approach, my soul, the Mercy
Seat', and 'Quiet, Lord, my froward heart'.

He never, any more than St Paul, lost his sense of amaze-
ment and gratitude at what Christ had done for him. He is
never happier than when he sings of the Saviour:

> No! I must my praises bring,
>   Though they worthless are and weak,
> For, should I refuse to sing,
>   Sure the very stones would speak.

No doubt, there are long stretches of dullness and doggerel. There are frequently expressions quaint to the verge of grotesqueness as in the last verse of 'Though troubles assail':

> When life sinks apace, And death is in view,
>   This word of His grace Shall comfort us through:
> No fearing or doubting; With Christ on our side,
>   We hope to die shouting, *The Lord will provide!*

There are faulty rhymes, too, as in almost every verse of 'Begone, Unbelief, my Saviour is near'.[1]

But what F. T. Palgrave says of another of the hymns,[2] 'In evil long I took delight, unawed by shame and fear', that its 'mere bare simplicity and sincerity suffice to range it amongst the most powerful', is true of many in the book as a whole.

The second attack of Cowper's malady broke out, and one winter night in 1773 he became raving mad. He was taken at his own request to the Vicarage hard by, and though in a little while he became calmer, he utterly refused to leave its

---

[1]   His love in time past
        Forbids me to think
      He'll leave me at last
        In trouble to sink;
      Each sweet Ebenezer
        I have in review,
      Confirms His good pleasure
        To help me quite through.
Of this we may say as Rendel Harris does of Robert Robinson's
      Here I raise my Ebenezer,
        Hither by Thine help I'm come,
      And I hope, by Thy good pleasure,
        Safely to arrive at home:
'All the rhymes may be challenged, and all the reasons are unchallengeable.' *As Pants the Hart*, p. 138.

[2] One wonders whether even in Olney Church or the Great House any one ever sang it.

shelter, and the Newtons had both him and his faithful companion Mrs Unwin living with them for a year. What the strain must have been, day after day, only those who have had something like the same experience can know.

Yet all that Newton permits himself to say is:

'Upon the whole I have not been weary of my cross. Besides the submission I owe to the Lord, I think I can hardly do or suffer too much for such a friend. Yet sometimes my heart has been impatient or rebellious.'

You have heard the 'faint praise' which Sir James Frazer grudgingly gives. Surely Sir James Stephen is nearer the truth:

'Newton . . . is the very counterpart of our old friend *Mr Greatheart*, beneath whose shield *Mr Feeble-Mind* and *Miss Much Afraid* found shelter, and before whose arm the walls of *Doubting Castle* and the might of *Giant Despair* were overthrown.'[1]

After all, when we think of the alternatives in the medical treatment of the insane in those days, and the horrors of Bedlam as one sees them depicted in Hogarth's ghastly picture in 'The Rake's Progress', we can only be thankful that in Olney Vicarage Cowper gained a refuge in his extremity which perhaps he would have found nowhere else in the world.

Jay of Bath says of John Newton:[2]

'He was the very man of all others I would have chosen for him. He was not rigid in his creed. His views of the Gospel were most free and encouraging. He had the tenderest disposition, and always judiciously regarded his friend's depression and despondency as a physical effect, for the removal of which he prayed, but never reasoned or argued with him concerning it.'

One thing further may be added. If we are to judge a man not only by his own writings but by what other men write *to* him, knowing the kind of things he would like to hear, and would appreciate to the full, we gain a reliable insight into his true character.

[1] Sir James Stephen, *Studies in Ecclesiastical Biography*, p. 411.
[2] William Jay of Bath, *Autobiography*, p. 280.

From many examples that might be quoted from Cowper's Letters, let the following suffice:

'Swift observes when he is giving his reasons why the preacher is elevated always above his hearers, that, let the crowd be as great as it will below, there is always room enough overhead. If the French philosophers can carry their art of flying to the perfection they desire, the observation may be reversed, the crowd will be overhead, and they will have most room who stay below. I can assure you, however, upon my own experience, that this way of travelling is very delightful. I dreamt a night or two since that I drove myself through the upper regions in a balloon and pair, with the greatest ease and security. Having finished the tour I intended, I made a short turn, and, with one flourish of my whip, descended; my horses prancing and curvetting with an infinite share of spirit, but without the least danger, either to me or my vehicle. The time, we may suppose, is at hand, and seems to be prognosticated by my dream, when these airy excursions will be universal, when judges will fly the circuit, and bishops their visitations; and when the tour of Europe will be performed with much greater speed, and with equal advantage, by all who travel for the sake of having it to say, that they have made it.'

'I never wrote a copy of Mary and John—

  (If John marries Mary and Mary alone,
   'Tis a very good match between Mary and John;
   Should John wed a score, oh! the claws and the scratches!
   It can't be a match: 'tis a bundle of matches.)—

in my life except that which I sent you. It was one of those bagatelles which sometimes spring up like mushrooms in my imagination either while I am writing or just before I begin. I sent it to you, because to you I send anything that I think may raise a smile.'

Or take this, from the well-known jingling *Hop-o'-my-Thumb* letter:

'The news at Oney is little or none-y, but such as it is I send it, viz. . . And now I have writ in a rhyming fit, what will make you dance, and as you advance will keep you still though against your will, dancing away alert and gay, till you come to an end of what I have penn'd; which that you may do ere

Madam and you are quite worn out with jigging about, I take my leave, and here you receive a bow profound down to the ground, from your humble me, W. C.'

These are extracts from letters written by Cowper to Newton. Of course, the letters are not all like these. Some are gloomy almost to the point of despair. But surely anything more grotesquely unlike the picture which Bagehot had drawn of a wretched timid slave cowering under the lash of his driver, could hardly be conceived.

Newton had now been a little over fifteen years at Olney—years, as we have seen, very varied in their experience. He was fifty-four, but his iron frame showed few of the signs of age. His friend, John Thornton of Clapham, who had already so handsomely subsidized his stipend at Olney, was patron of the Church and parish of St Mary Woolnoth, London, and the very day after the death of its old incumbent, Dr Plumptre, 18 September 1779, he wrote offering his cure to Newton, who three days later accepted it. In a characteristic letter to Bull, Newton writes:

'My race at Olney is nearly finished. I am about to form a connexion in life with one Mary Woolnoth, a reputed London saint in Lombard Street. . . I am not elated at what the world calls preferment. The throng and hurry of the busy world and noise and party contentions of the religious world are very disagreeable to me. I love woods and fields and streams and trees —to hear the birds sing and sheep bleat. . . I am sure no outward change can make me happier, but it becomes not a soldier to choose his own post.'

There were some difficulties, both as to the appointment of his successor in Olney and his own settlement in London, and it was not till 13 January 1780 that he preached for the last time in the Great House, for the dedication of which, eleven years before, he and Cowper had written two of their best known hymns: 'Dear Shepherd of Thy people, hear', and 'Jesus, where'er Thy people meet'.

There is a pathetic letter from Cowper in which he says:

'The vicarage house became a melancholy object as soon as Mr Newton left it. As I walked in the garden this evening, I

saw the smoke issue from the study chimney and said to myself, "that used to be a sign that Mr Newton was there": but
it is so no longer. The walls of the house know nothing of the
change that has taken place: the bolt of the chamber door
sounds just as it used to do; and when Mr Page goes upstairs,
for aught I know or ever shall know, the fall of his foot could
hardly perhaps be distinguished from that of Mr Newton. But
Mr Newton's foot will never be heard upon that staircase
again.'

St Mary Woolnoth, under the new ministry, soon became
one of the chief centres of the Evangelical Movement in London. It is a comparatively small church, and at present can
hold only about three hundred people. In Newton's time galleries, long since removed, would provide sittings for perhaps
half as many again. He was never run after as a popular
preacher except at first, when some of his parishioners grum-
bled at their seats being taken by strangers who would even
crowd the aisles, much to the annoyance of some of the city
bankers who still lived above their offices in Lombard Street.
One of them proposed to Newton that he should allow another
clergyman to preach occasionally for him, since, if it was uncertain whether the rector was to be on duty or not, people
would not throng the church so much! He said of himself, 'I
hope I am upon the whole a Scriptural preacher: for I find I
am considered as an Arminian among the high Calvinists and
as a Calvinist among the strenuous Arminians.'[1]

[1] In one of his letters, 10 September 1771, to Mr C. (Cecil?), he gives some
of his views on preaching: 'There is still in being an old-fashioned instru-
ment called an hour-glass which in days of yore, before clocks and watches
abounded, used to be the measure of many a good sermon, and I think it a
tolerable stint. I cannot wind up my ends to my own satisfaction in a much
shorter time, nor am I pleased with myself if I greatly exceed it. If an angel
was to preach for two hours, unless his hearers were angels likewise, I believe the greater part of them would wish he had done. It is a shame it
should be so, but so it is; partly through the weakness, and partly through
the wickedness of the flesh, we can seldom stretch our attention to spiritual
things for two hours together without cracking it, and hurting its spring;
and when weariness begins, edification ends. Perhaps it is better to feed our
people like chickens, a little and often, than to cram them like turkeys, till

Yet he had his own place and power not only because he was
'Minister of the first parish of the first magistrate of the first
city in the world', but because his life-story was well known. I
suppose that neither before nor since his day has there ever
been any incumbent of a London city charge who bore on his
back the scars of the navy 'Cat'. Men into whose soul the iron
had entered, turned naturally to St Mary Woolnoth, and found
in Newton's preaching medicine and healing for their wounds.

His parish duties were not specially heavy, though of course
the City at the close of the eighteenth century was still a resi-
dential part of London. John Gilpin and his wife and children
three, we remember, lived not five minutes' walk distant in
Cheapside over the shop, ready for all customers coming in;
and 'Merry Islington' was still a village on the outskirts of the
town. Pastoral visitation was confined within a comparatively
narrow area, and there was an almost complete absence of the
meetings that engulf the afternoons and evenings of a minister's life to-day. But the English clergyman then—especially if
he was an Evangelical—was expected to give himself body and
soul to preaching; and we hear that, either in his own church
or helping his brethren, Newton would frequently in those
early years of his London ministry preach as often as six times
in the week.

His hymn-writing practically ceased after Olney, and any
verses written in London have no poetic merit whatever. On
the other hand, he found scope for a wider ministry than any
he had known hitherto, in a perfect cataract of correspondence.
People of all sorts made him their father-confessor, laying bare
to him the secrets of their souls; and, no matter who the writer
might be, every letter was patiently and fully answered.

He never set much store by his preaching. 'As for my
letters, it was the Lord's will that I should do most by them.'

Much of this correspondence is barely readable now, and

they cannot hold one gobbet more. Besides, over-long sermons break in
upon family concerns, and often call off the thoughts from the sermon to
the pudding at home, which is in danger of being over-boiled. They leave
likewise but little time for secret or family religion, which are both very good
in their place, and are entitled to a share in the Lord's Day.' *Works*, p. 343.

the language is conventional. There is nothing of the lyrical
fire and imagination that one finds in Samuel Rutherford,
nothing of the subtlety and knowledge of the human soul that
some of the great doctors in the Roman Church display. But
Newton has his own merits. Though many of his correspondents are women, he is entirely free from all self-consciousness
or sentimentality or lusciousness of expression. *Cardiphonia* still
keeps its place as a devotional classic, and one never reads far
without feeling in close contact with a transparently honest,
robust-minded, good man, gifted with excellent common
sense, and with humour and that unwearied patience and
loving-kindness whose worth Cowper had proved at Olney.

No doubt Newton wrote too easily and published too much,
and in all he wrote he had edification as his main end. But I
cannot assent to Lord David Cecil's opinion in his admirable
Life of Cowper—*The Stricken Deer*, one of the finest biographical studies written in the last thirty years—that the
*Authentic Narrative of some Interesting Particulars in the Life of John
Newton* is 'a fusty, forbidding little book, and more than half of
it is pious platitude'. Distaste for the kind of experience the
Narrative records and for its theological presuppositions may
easily disqualify for appreciation of the vitality and vigour
which animate it, and, perhaps also, of the excellence of the
English this self-taught man had learned to write. Newton's
personality infuses interest into much less prepossessing subjects. Even his Sermons, though not marked in any way by
eloquence, are couched in an admirably plain, robust, manly
speech, and are not infrequently relieved from dullness by the
play of a curious sardonic humour. 'The style is the man
himself.'

During these years in London Newton had many sorrows in
his home. The childless couple had adopted two nieces of Mrs
Newton's, Eliza Cunningham and Betsy Catlett. The former,
always a delicate child, early developed signs of consumption,
and died in 1785, when she was not yet fifteen years of age.
Newton wrote, after the manner of that day, an almost pain-
fully detailed narrative of her last illness and dying sayings and
death. It would be easy to censure as morbid this and the type

E

of early piety therein displayed, but the genuine goodness and tenderness of the writer shine out on every page. Of the other niece, Betsy Catlett, I shall speak presently.

In the year 1788 Mrs Newton, who had been in poor health for a long time, discovered after a visit to a surgeon that she was suffering from cancer, the result of an accident more than twenty years previously, and that the malady was too far advanced for any remedy that the skill of the time could provide. For two years she endured an almost constantly increasing suffering, and during part of the time mental darkness and despair clouded her reason. Happily this passed, and when the end came, 15 December 1790, there was peace. Here, too, Newton has left a long and pathetic narrative. It is significant of the type of man he was that, on the very day of his wife's death, when she lay unconscious, he went to church and preached, and, on the day following, 'I was afraid of sitting at home and indulging myself by poring over my loss: and therefore I was seen in the street, and visited some of my serious friends. I likewise preached three times while she lay dead in the house. Some of my brethren kindly offered their assistance; but as the Lord was pleased to give me strength both of body and mind, I thought it my duty to stand up in my place as formerly.' On the following Sunday he preached her funeral sermon. Every year till his own death seventeen years afterwards, he spent the anniversary in absolute seclusion and recollection, and wrote a series of pathetic little elegies in her memory.

Such self-repression may seem strange and repellent, but at least it was no Stoic *Apathy* at the touch of which, as Seeley says, the Christian temper has always shivered.[1]

For eleven years after his wife's death, her niece Betsy Cat-

---

[1] Undoubtedly Dr John Brown has said the last word here: 'Such things are not right: they are a cruelty and injustice and injury from the soul to the body, its faithful slave, and they bring down . . . their own certain and specific retribution. A man who did not feel keenly might have preached: a man whose whole nature was torn, shattered and astonished as his was, had, in a high sense, no right so to use himself.' Dr John Brown, 'Letter to John Cairns, D.D.' in *Horae Subsecivae*, 2nd Series.

lett was a true daughter to Newton, and then her health, too, broke down. She was removed to Bethlem Hospital, where she remained under treatment for about two years. This illness was a terrible trial to the man who had borne up so marvellously at his wife's death. His sight had failed, but every morning at a certain hour he insisted on being led to the street close by the Asylum, underneath the window of the ward where his niece was. Pointing to the window, he would ask his attendant, 'Do you see a white handkerchief being waved to and fro?' and being assured of the signal which he could not see, the old man would turn and go home content. Happily the treatment proved successful. Betsy gained complete health, returned home, and in due course married happily and survived her uncle many years.

During these later years in London, till his faculties began to fail, Newton became the leading figure in the Evangelical circles of the time. He was one of the founders, in 1783, of the Eclectic Society, out of which sprang the Church Missionary Society. It was also his custom once a week to give breakfasts —a favourite form of entertainment in the earlier part of last century, as every reader of Macaulay's Life will remember; and at these functions young men in the ministry and in training for it were specially welcome.[1] William Jay of Bath has left us a very pleasant account of some of those gatherings, and of the racy sayings of the old veteran and his cordial friendliness to his juniors.

'These breakfasts (he says) were attended by ministers and Christians of all denominations. Then would come family worship and after the reading of the chapter he would add a

---

[1] Dr Alexander Waugh of Wells Street 'used frequently to introduce to Newton such of his Scottish brethren as happened to visit London and who were naturally anxious to see that distinguished writer and excellent man. On one of those occasions Mr Waugh said, "Well, Sir, I have brought another of my northern friends to see you." "Ah, my brother," said the venerable Newton, "I was once a wild lion of the coast of Africa: there God took me and turned me and brought me to London; and now you come to see me as they do the lions in the Tower." ' *Memoir of Dr Waugh*, by Hay and Belfrage, p. 112.

few remarks, very brief, but weighty and striking. He always prayed himself, never long, but remarkably suitable, and simple. After service and breakfast he withdrew to his study with any of his male friends who could remain for a while, and there with his pipe (the only pipe I ever liked, except Robert Hall's) he would converse in a manner the most free and varied and delightful and edifying. Nothing about him was dull or gloomy or puritanical according to the common meaning of the term . . . Sometimes he had the strangest fetches of drollery. Thus one day by a strong sneeze he shook off a fly which had perched on his *gnomon*, and immediately said, "Now if this fly keeps a diary, he'll write, *Today a terrible earthquake.*" At another time when I asked him how he slept, he instantly replied, "I'm like a beef-steak—once turned and I'm done."

'Of his sayings I can remember that when he was talking on the choice of texts, he said to a certain Baptist minister much given to proselytising, 'Ah, Brother, there is one text *I* can preach from, and that *you* cannot.' 'Sir, what can that be?' 'Christ sent me not to baptise, but to preach the Gospel.' Again, 'Some people believe much better than they argue. I once heard a good old woman arguing in favour of eternal election. "Sir," said she, "I'm sure if God had not chosen me before I was born, He would never have chosen me after." ' [1]

Small beer these recollections may be. But they give us an idea of the man very different from the ogre of Sir James Frazer's fancy. And one thing more may be added—the love that little children and the childless old man had for each other.[2] Jay has this anecdote: 'I recollect a little sailor boy calling upon him with his father. Mr Newton soon noticed him, and taking him between his knees, he told him he had been much at sea himself, and then sang part of a naval song.' Josiah Bull, in his *Life of Newton*, mentions that he himself once happened to be amusing some little ones by making small paper boats. "Ah," said his father, sitting by and showing great

---

[1] Jay, loc. cit., pp. 287–9.

[2] At Olney he once wrote: 'I see in this world two heaps of human happiness and misery: now if I can take but the smallest bit from one heap and add it to the other I carry a point—if as I go home, a child has dropped a halfpenny and by giving it another I can wipe away its tears, I feel I have done something.'

interest in the matter, "Mr Newton used to make just such
boats as these to please me when I was a child, and I have
never seen any like them since."

' "I charge you," says Newton in one of his letters to his friend
Mr Bull, "I charge you upon your allegiance that you bring
Tommy [his son, eight years old] with you when you come to
London. Venture not into my presence without him. We shall
find some auger-hole in which to put him." Once more, in a
letter to Betsy Catlett, aged fourteen, at school, we find him
writing this: "I remember when you were a little girl at North-
ampton School—I found such an affection for you that I would
not part with you for your weight in gold. And though you are
much heavier now than you were then, I can say the same
still." '

Newton lived long enough to see and take part in the revival
of Missionary Enterprise that followed the departure of William Carey to India. Writing to his friend, Dr Claudius
Buchanan, who had gone out to India holding a valuable
ecclesiastical appointment, and who had seemed at first to be
very shy of the Baptist missionaries,[1] he says: 'It is easy for you
(little as yet tried in character, and from your superior and
patronized station) to look down upon men who have given
themselves to the Lord, and are bearing the burden and heat
of the day. I do not look for miracles, but if God were to work
one in our day, I should not wonder if it were in favour of Dr
Carey.'[2]

He also, as we have seen, wrote a very striking paper,
Thoughts upon the African Slave Trade, with the Golden Rule as
motto, and the well-known tag from Terence, *Homo Sum*; and
he took a notable part in the early days of the anti-Slavery
Movement along with Wilberforce and Zachary Macaulay.
This paper is strictly and studiously moderate in its tone, but
nothing could be more damning as an indictment of 'a commerce so iniquitous, so cruel, so oppressive, so destructive as

---

[1] We remember Sydney Smith's sneering reference to 'consecrated
cobblers'.
[2] Jay, p. 279.

the African Slave Trade'. 'I have written' (he says) 'from a
conviction that the share I have formerly had in the trade
binds me in conscience to throw what light I am able upon the
subject, now it is likely to become a point of parliamentary
investigation.'

The last two years of Newton's life were marked by great and
increasing feebleness, loss of sight, hearing, memory, and voice.
But he still insisted on taking his turn in preaching, one of the
City Aldermen regularly sending his carriage to drive him the
short distance from his house in Coleman Street close by the
Guildhall to St Mary Woolnoth. Like John Knox in the Town
Church at St Andrews, he needed to be helped up the stairs to
the pulpit under its great sounding board, but once there he
would preach with much of his old animation. 'Stop?' he
once said to his friend and biographer, Richard Cecil, who
hinted to him that 'in the article of public preaching it might
be best for you to consider your work as done and stop before
you evidently discover you can speak no longer'; 'I cannot
stop', raising his voice, 'What! Shall the old African blas-
phemer stop while he can speak?'

But the day came when this was no longer possible. Friends
came to see him in his room, but often he was barely conscious
of them or would merely stretch out his hand in recognition if
they prayed with him. At other times he would say with something of his old grave waggishness, 'I am like a person going a
journey in a stage-coach who expects its arrival every hour,
and is frequently looking out of the window for it—I am
packed and sealed and ready for the post.'

We owe this final glimpse of him to William Jay: 'I saw Mr
Newton near the closing scene. He was hardly able to talk:
and all I had noted down upon my leaving him is this: "My
memory is nearly gone, but I remember two things: That I am
a great sinner, and that Christ is a great Saviour." ' He had
once said when he heard some one asking particularly about
the last words of an eminent believer, 'Tell me not how the
man died, but how he lived,' and he himself spoke very little
on his deathbed—in strong contrast to that quaint aspiration
in the Olney Hymns, twenty-eight years before:

We hope to die shouting *The Lord will provide!*

His last recorded words to one who asked him if his mind was comfortable were, 'I am satisfied with the Lord's will.' This was the old man's *Nunc Dimittis*, 21 December 1807.

On the last day of the year his coffin was placed beside that of his wife in the vault underneath St Mary's Church, and the marble tablet with its so characteristic inscription was duly set on the wall beside the vestry door. But Newton's body does not remain in its first resting-place. The exigencies of metropolitan transport have diverted city traffic more and more from the narrow congested streets to the very depths of London clay. The South London Tube has burrowed its way under the foundations of church and Bank and Mansion House, and set one of its stations directly underneath St Mary Woolnoth. In 1893 the coffins of John Newton and Mary Catlett his wife were removed in reverence from the crypt and taken to Olney. There they were buried hard by the church and the Great House and all the other well-remembered spots that the pilgrim will ever associate with their names and with that of their dear friend who owed so much to them, alike in days of darkness and of light, William Cowper.

THE CONSTITUENTS OF A GOOD HYMN

THIS subject may seem at first sight a very simple one. Even the man in the street has his own ideas about a hymn—at least about the kind of hymn which he likes; and the B.B.C., from St Martin's-in-the-Fields and other Regional centres, is ready to give him all he wishes. It will be worth our while, however, to go a step or two further, and not only form a judgement on 'The Constituents of a Good Hymn', but be prepared to give our reasons and justify our opinion. It all seems quite simple, until we begin to examine and cross-question our own ideas, as well as the different definitions of a hymn that have been given in quarters to which we owe respect. *Then* we begin to realize how hard it is, in David Deans's words, to 'keep the true testimony, and the middle and straight path, as it were, on the ridge of a hill, where wind and water shears, avoiding right-hand snares and extremes, and left-hand way-slidings.' Yet surely the attempt ought to be made—if for no other reason than that most laudable one of clearing one's own mind.

When we come to consider the question in its various aspects, we see that it is no mere matter of definition. We must not forthwith assume that no other criteria can or ought to be applied than those we bring to the judgement of poetry. The story is told somewhere of Matthew Arnold that in the course of one of his prelections as Professor of Poetry at Oxford, he held up first a copy of Palgrave's *Golden Treasury*, and then Roundell Palmer's *The Book of Praise*, and said, 'Why is it that *this* contains almost nothing that is bad, and *that* almost nothing that is good?' The story—good as it is, *qua* story—is almost more illuminating in its revelation of the critic and his peculiar limitations than as a contribution to the elucidation of the subject. The Hymn has its distinctive place, not only in the realm of poetry, but as an integral and essential part of the worship which man offers to God, and therefore it must be judged by other tests than those which apply to poetry alone.

'A Hymn', says the great *Oxford Dictionary*, 'is a song of praise to God: any composition in praise of God which is

adapted to be chanted or sung; specially a metrical composition adapted to be sung in a religious service; sometimes distinguished from *Psalm* or *Anthem* as not being part of the text of
the Bible.' Etymologically, the word is pure Greek: ὕμνος—a
song or ode in praise of gods or heroes . . . sometimes in epic
form as in the Homeric or Orphic Hymns, but more usually in
Lyric, as those of Pindar—the latter being properly sung to the
Cithara without dancing.'

I am not sufficiently acquainted with those different types
of classical hymn to say anything about them that would be to
the purpose. But there can be no doubt that Dr T. R. Glover
is right when he speaks of 'the *new note* that is heard in the
words of the early Christians. Stoicism was never "essentially
musical"; Epictetus announces a hymn to Zeus, but he never
starts the tune. Over and over again there is a sound of singing
in Paul—as in the eighth chapter of the Romans and the thir-
teenth of First Corinthians, and it repeats itself.' As the late
Bishop Frere finely said, 'The Christian Church may be said
to have started on its way singing.' What was thus begun has
never ceased.

I need not quote the familiar passage from Pliny's letter to
Trajan about the customs of primitive Christians in their worship, or tell over again the well-known stories of the use of
hymns in the great days of Ambrose, and the influence that
they had in the spiritual history of Augustine. What is of
special interest to us in our present study is a note in the latter's
commentary on the seventy-second psalm, in which he gives
his definition of a hymn: 'Hymns are praises of God with
singing; hymns are songs containing praises of God. If there be
praise and not praise of God, it is not a hymn. If there be
praise and praise of God and it is not sung, it is not a hymn. It
is necessary therefore, if it be a hymn, that it have these three
things: both praise, and praise of God, and that it be sung.'
There is no lack of clearness and even rigour here. As a definition of a hymn, it would entirely fall in with the ideas of Lord
Hugh Cecil[1] who, as I am informed, since his appointment as
Provost of Eton, prescribes for use in the School Chapel only

[1] Now Lord Quickswood.

such hymns as are addressed to God in direct praise and prayer.

Such a definition, however, is much too narrow. There are hymns of meditation and description, of exhortation and teaching. There is the glorious outburst of praise—and how much else!—in Milton's *Hymn* (his own word for it, though so many people persist in calling it an *Ode*) *on the Morning of Christ's Nativity*. I do not think it is possible to come to any particular hymn—or any collection of hymns—with any hard-and-fast definition of *what it ought to be*. If you do, you almost inevitably land yourself in a perfect morass of confused thinking, such as that in which one generally accurate and competent critic[1] flounders when he writes: 'Not only is a hymn not necessarily poetry and not necessarily theology (though very often it is both): it is not *necessarily* anything—provided only that it lends itself to the common worship of God by words and music. There is no such thing as the hymn-in-itself. The same composition can be a hymn at one time, and something else (as an anthem or responsive prayer) at another.' This, it seems to me, if it means anything at all, means simply: 'A hymn's a hymn, and there's an end on't'; which, of course, is true, but which, equally of course, does not carry one much further.

But a *good* hymn and its constituents, which, after all, is our subject; the qualities which it must possess if it is to be *good* in any real intelligible sense: *that*, surely, should be something which the mind can grasp, and common, everyday language can express.

The first thing we look for in a good hymn is that *it should be about something definite*—a thought, a feeling, a statement—something that has a beginning, a middle, and, if possible, an end. Many so-called hymns are wanting in these very respects —particularly the last; wandering on vaguely, with no particular object or climax. How they have begun, we know not; why and when—if ever—they should end, is no less mysterious. Luther's famous characterization of what a sermon ought to be is equally true of a hymn: 'I endeavour in my sermons to take a text, and to keep to it, and so to show it to the people and spread it out before them, that they may say, "*This* is what

[1] Rev. Arthur S. Gregory, in *Praises with Understanding*.

the sermon is about."' An interesting parallel to this may be
found in the remark of a lady who had heard John Wesley
preach: 'Is this the great Mr Wesley of whom we hear so
much at the present day? Why, the poorest person in the
chapel could have understood him!'

This is a very searching, but surely not at all an unreasonable, test to apply to a hymn. I wonder if some of our popular
hymns would stand it. Take, for instance, Faber's 'Hark, hark,
my soul, angelic songs are swelling.' It is all very melodious.
There are lines in it which, taken by themselves, are quite
intelligible. There are pictures and impressions of certain sights
and sounds. There is at times a real surge of emotion. But as to
what it all *means*, what *purpose* it is intended to serve, I am
afraid we are like Abner: 'As thy soul liveth, O King, I cannot
tell.'

If there were a more definite idea in the minds of the perpe-
trators of so many hymns as to what they really wished to say,
there would at once be a slackening in the flood of composition
which threatens to inundate the land. The writing of a good
hymn, far from being the easy thing which so many who
attempt the task imagine it to be—the occupation of an otherwise idle afternoon—is even more difficult than the composing
of a sonnet. For one thing, the metrical framework of a hymn
is less rigid and therefore gives less support. The rule which
Southey laid down for the writing of an epitaph—'Think as
much as possible about what you have to say, and as little as
possible about the manner of saying it'—is the first and great
commandment for all would-be hymn-writers.

It seems to me that the only satisfactory way of reaching a
conclusion as to the constituents of a good hymn is as far as
possible to lay aside presuppositions. Take certain hymns universally acknowledged to be in the front rank. Examine and
analyse these, if necessary, line by line, or even word by word,
as well as in their broad general effect, and see if, by any
means, they will yield their secret. Take, for instance, such
hymns as Watts's 'O God, our help in ages past' and 'When I
survey the wondrous Cross', Charles Wesley's 'Jesu, Lover of
my soul', Toplady's 'Rock of ages, cleft for me', Heber's

'Holy, holy, holy, Lord God Almighty', Lyte's 'Abide with me, fast falls the eventide'.

The selection is almost random, but every one, expert and common man, knows these to be hymns in the front rank. No committee of selection would so much as dream of omitting them from any proposed hymn-book. Every line of them is familiar—not so much from any pure poetic quality (one would be surprised to find them in any anthology of English poetry) as from a certain quality different from, and deeper than, what mere literature can supply.

In the first of these hymns, then, 'O God, our help in ages past,' Watts has, unquestionably and emphatically, *something to say*, and he loses no time in saying it with the utmost strength, simplicity, and dignity. When it is remembered that the hymn was written in the closing days of the life of Queen Anne, at a time when the air was thick with the rumour of Jacobite plot and counter-plot and no one could say what the morrow would bring, one has a new sense of the steadfast unselfconscious faith of the writer. There is no weak or unworthy line in the entire hymn. The images in verse after verse leave an absolutely clean-cut impression. We remember the fourth verse:

> A thousand ages in Thy sight
> Are like an evening gone,
> Short as the watch that ends the night
> Before the rising sun—

twenty-three words, eighteen of them monosyllables—and the fifth and sixth:

> The busy tribes of flesh and blood,
> With all their lives and cares,
> Are carried downwards by the flood
> And lost in following years.

> Time, like an ever-rolling stream,
> Bears all its sons away,
> They fly forgotten, as a dream
> Dies at the opening day.

One hammer-stroke follows upon another: and we ask, Were

ever the great, simple commonplaces of human experience described more adequately? And yet, as a hymn, there is something lacking in it: the passion and ardour which will not be restrained, but which has nothing weak, or shallow, or merely emotional in it. *This* element we find in every verse and line of 'When I survey the wondrous Cross.' Of course the atmosphere here is entirely different from that of the psalm, but the words and epithets here are as absolutely right: 'survey', 'compose', 'amazing', 'divine'. One could not imagine any of these being altered or improved.

But not even in such a hymn was it given to Watts to keep from over-emphasis. He himself, on revision, struck out what he had written in his first draft:

> Where the young Prince of Glory died;

and the fourth verse of the original:

> His dying crimson like a robe
>   Spread o'er His body on the tree;
> Then am I dead to all the globe,
>   And all the globe is dead to me—

startlingly vivid as the opening image is, was marked with brackets for omission. This, too, one feels, was a case of second thoughts being best, though the omitted verse is retained, of all places in the world, in *Songs of Praise*. I need scarcely add that the fussy and irrelevant Doxology in *Hymns Ancient and Modern*,

> To Christ Who won for sinners grace
>   By bitter grief and anguish sore,
> Be praise from all the ransom'd race
>   For ever and for ever more,—

a complete anti-climax after the passion of adoring gratitude,

> Love so amazing, so divine,
>   Demands my soul, my life, my all—

is an effort of the compilers. Heaven knows what they meant; what they found lacking.

In its concentration and restrained strength, what a contrast

the whole hymn presents to that other well-known hymn
for Good Friday, Faber's appeal to the emotions, 'O come and
mourn with me awhile!' No doubt in this hymn there are fine
lines, as in almost everything that Faber wrote. But can one
conceive anything, as a whole, more alien to the whole New
Testament view of the Cross, and its message to sinful men?

Isaac Watts's genius is for the most part pedestrian, firm as
is the stride. Only rarely does it take to itself wings. In Charles
Wesley at his best, on the other hand, this is repeatedly the
case. Take practically the whole of 'Jesu, Lover of my soul' or
of 'Come, O Thou Traveller unknown', which Watts mag-
nanimously declared to be 'worth all the verses he himself had
written'. Think of the magical third and fourth lines: simplicity
itself, but of imagination all compact:

> My company before is gone,
> And I am left alone with Thee.

Another characteristic of Charles Wesley's genius is the way
in which he will weave together passage after passage of Scripture. For instance, in the sixteen lines of his noble hymn:

> O Thou Who camest from above
> The pure celestial fire to impart,

it has been pointed out that there are no fewer than twenty-
three allusions to, or direct citations from, Scripture. Or again,
in each of the four lines, still more familiar,

> Thou of life the fountain art,
>   Freely let me take of Thee;
> Spring Thou up within my heart,
>   Rise to all eternity—

we have a definite text: 'With Thee is the fountain of life';
'Let him take of the water of life freely'; 'Spring up, O well';
'The water that I shall give him shall be in him a well of
water springing up into everlasting life.'

In yet another hymn of Wesley's we see this same faculty
now taking a whole incident: the narrative of Peter's escape
from prison:

> Long my imprison'd spirit lay
>   Fast bound in sin and nature's night;
> Thine eye diffused a quick'ning ray;
>   I woke, the dungeon flam'd with light;
> My chains fell off, my heart was free,—
>   I rose, went forth, and follow'd Thee.

All through there is heard no stammering quotation, but the authentic 'lyric cry'.

Take as another example for examination perhaps the best known hymn in the English language, which Saintsbury in his *English Prosody* calls 'this really great poem, whose every word, every syllable, has its place and meaning', Augustus Montague Toplady's 'Rock of Ages, cleft for me'. No doubt, if one were to analyse it line after line, it would be easy to reduce the entire hymn to a heap of inconsistent and constantly changing metaphors: the Rock which is a 'hiding-place' and yet 'cleft'; the 'riven side', the 'double cure'; the 'cleansing' from 'power', as well as from 'guilt'. The second verse is a paraphrase of some verses from the Epistle to the Romans. In the third the images and metaphors reappear: 'clinging to the Cross' in nakedness and helplessness, 'flying to the fountain' there to be 'washed'. In the fourth verse we have the almost ghastly realism of Toplady's original,

> When my eye-strings break in death,

the Resurrection from the dead, and the Last Judgement, and the final repose of the ransomed soul. Yet, while all the confusion of the scattered fragments may be granted, somehow, when the severest, most destructive analysis has done its utmost, the hymn gathers and knits itself together, not only refusing to die, but thrilling with new life by the sheer force of its reality and sincerity and passion, expressing the deepest, most universal feelings in religious experience.

So one might go on, examining and analysing hymn after hymn, 'Abide with me, fast falls the eventide'—almost perfect in its expression, and with lines in it like

> Swift to its close ebbs out life's little day,

which any poet might have been proud—or thankful—to have written, and whose sheer beauty survives—nay, triumphs over —the final indignity of community singing at a Cup football tie.

Or again, the 'lonely and austere adoration' of Heber's hymn for Trinity Sunday, 'Holy, holy, holy, Lord God Almighty!'— a whole system of Dogmatic Theology, but possessing that essential in a Creed—that *it can be sung.*

As a result of our examination and analysis of hymns which are universally acknowledged to be good, and far more than good in the strictest sense of the term, can we deduce any principles which will guide us to a sound judgement as to *what are the constituents of a good hymn,* and also as to *the elements which should* NOT *be found in any hymn described as good?*

I think we can. *Something to say,* in the first instance, and then, in the way of saying it—such absolutely essential characteristics as *Sincerity, Simplicity, Reverence, Fervour, the Glow of Imagination,* all controlled in their expression and interpenetrated by Scripture: these on the *positive* side; and on the *negative,* the *absence of anything merely facile or conventional or sentimental,* any *mere ornament for ornament's sake,* anything *clever or self-conscious,* or *cheap and vulgar.* Such, positively and negatively, are the chief characteristics of the hymns we have been considering, hymns which have stood the test of time, and whose message is practically independent of any merely *temporal* or *spatial,* even as they are of *national* and *ecclesiastical* factors. We never think of asking, when we sing such hymns, what church connection their writers had. We are well content to ignore or forget such irrelevances as the bitter quarrels and the scurrilous words that passed between Toplady and Wesley, remembering only the common gift that each gave to the Church.

One element that we noticed as being so marked in those hymns—their *Scripturalness*—is due, no doubt, to the place which the Psalms held in public worship. If in one respect this was a narrowing influence, it certainly saved the praise of the Church in our land from the extravagance and bad taste which so greatly mar many German hymns, especially those of the Pietist school, and the Moravian most of all.

In England this Scripturalness is seen to the fullest extent in the famous little collection *Olney Hymns* (1779) by John Newton and William Cowper. The first of the three books into which it is divided contains one hundred and forty-one hymns, expressly written on or around definite passages of Scripture; the other two, hymns composed for special occasions, and on subjects connected with Christian experience. Newton—I may remark in passing, a greatly misunderstood and often maligned man— had a very sane and modest estimate of his own qualifications as a hymn-writer: 'There is a style and manner suited to the composition of hymns which may be more successfully, or at least more easily, attained by a versifier than by a poet. . . Perspicuity, simplicity, and ease should be chiefly attended to: and the imagery . . . of poetry if admitted at all should be indulged very sparingly, and with great judgement. . . If the Lord whom I serve has been pleased to favour me with that mediocrity of talent which may qualify me for usefulness to the weak and poor of His flock, without quite disgusting persons of superior discernment, I have reason to be satisfied.'

But now, passing from what Matthew Arnold calls 'our excellent and indispensable eighteenth-century', we see *a new influence* at work in hymns and hymn-writers, which has made itself more and more felt ever since. This is not very easy to define, but we see it in every collection of hymns from Bishop Heber, the 'creator of the modern hymn-book',[1] to the present day. It was *a new note* in praise that was heard in the now familiar lines:

> Waft, waft, ye winds, His story,
>   And you, ye waters, roll!
> Till, like a sea of glory,
>   It spreads from pole to pole.

The same note sounds in the famous lyric which, only six months after Scott's death, the compilers of an obscure Scottish collection, *Hymns adapted for the Worship of God, selected and*

---

[1] W. H. Frere: Introduction to the Historical Edition (1904) of *Hymns Ancient and Modern.*

F

sanctioned by the Synod of Relief, had the boldness and discernment to take over from *Ivanhoe*:

> By day, along the astonished lands
>   The cloudy pillar glided slow;
> By night, Arabia's crimsoned sands
>   Returned the fiery column's glow.

Again you have it in James Montgomery's noble lines:

> Arabia's desert ranger
>   To Him shall bow the knee;
> The Ethiopian stranger
>   His glory come to see;
> With offerings of devotion
>   Ships from the isles shall meet,
> To pour the wealth of ocean
>   In tribute at His feet.

No student of the subject needs to be reminded how often that unmistakable note is heard in many a hymn of Keble and Newman and Isaac Williams, and their successors—as genuine a product of what is rather loosely called the 'Romantic Movement' as anything in the greater poets of the day.

Of course, there is everything to be said for good poetry and bold imagery, the unhackneyed epithet, the vivid phrase, in the songs we sing in the sanctuary of God. It may indeed be urged that there can hardly be too much colour and picturesqueness in the wording of a hymn, if for no other reason than to give the worshipper the opportunity of exercising his imagination and feeling the thrill of something beyond his usual experience. But there is the obvious danger of introducing ornament for ornament's sake, and of allowing eloquence to degenerate into rhetoric, and even rant. We are only too conscious of this in certain modern hymns—more especially those from America; for instance, in W. C. Gannett's

> The Lord is in His holy place
>   In all things near and far,
> Shekinah of the snowflake He,
>   And Glory of the star—

which requires a footnote to make it intelligible to all but
Hebrew scholars; or in Julia Ward Howe's 'Battle Hymn of the
Republic':

> In the beauty of the lilies Christ was born across the sea,
> With a glory in His bosom that transfigures you and me;

or, to take a still better known instance, in Whittier's fine poem
'The Eternal Goodness', which, whatever its Quaker author
may have intended, finds a place as a hymn in many modern
collections:

> And so beside the silent sea
> I wait the muffled oar,

and again,

> I know not where His islands lift
> Their fronded palms in air—

a curious blending of Avernus and Polynesia! Whittier was
here forgetting his own wise caution, expressed in a striking
poem, 'The Brewing of Soma'.[1]

> They drank, and lo! in heart and brain
> A new, glad life began;
> The gray of hair grew young again,
> The sick man laughed away his pain,
> The cripple leaped and ran.
>
> As in that child-world's early year,
> Each after age has striven
> By music, incense, vigils drear,
> And trance, to bring the skies more near,
> Or lift men up to heaven!
>
> And yet the past comes round again,
> And new doth old fulfil;
> In sensual transports, wild as vain,
> We brew in many a Christian fane
> The heathen soma still!

---

[1] 'Soma' is an intoxicating liquor brewed from a plant of that name, by
drinking which the worshippers of Indra hoped to reach union with the
Deity.

> Dear Lord and Father of Mankind,
> Forgive our foolish ways!
> Reclothe us in our rightful mind,
> In purer lives Thy service find,
> In deeper reverence, praise.

Surely here we have the true maxim for all who would write
—or sing—hymns!

It is very interesting in connection with this part of our subject to read the Prefaces to different hymn-books. By far the
most racy and pertinent is John Wesley's to that famous 'little
body of experimental and practical divinity', *A Collection of
Hymns for use of the People called Methodists*: 'As but a small part
of these hymns is of my own composing, I do not think it inconsistent with modesty to declare that I am persuaded no such
hymn book as this has yet been published in the English language. In what other publication of the kind have you so
distinct and full an account of scriptural Christianity? such a
declaration of the heights and depths of religion, speculative
and practical? so strong cautions against the most plausible
errors; particularly those that are now most prevalent? and so
clear directions for making your calling and election sure; for
perfecting holiness in the fear of God? . . . In these hymns there
is no doggerel; no botches: nothing put in to patch up the
rhyme; no feeble expletives. Here is nothing turgid or bom-
bast, on the one hand, or low and creeping on the other. Here
are no *cant* expressions; no words without meaning. . . We talk
common sense, both in prose and verse, and use no word but in
a fixed and determinate sense. Here are, allow me to say, both
the purity, the strength, and the elegance of the English language; and, at the same time, the utmost simplicity and plain-
ness, suited to every capacity.'

It is quite plain that no writer of a publisher's 'blurb'
nowadays could have taught John Wesley anything! Indeed, I
cannot remember such a self-complacent preliminary statement ever being matched till the late Dr Dearmer took pen in
hand to set forth the merits of *Songs of Praise*! Yet it must be
admitted that a hymn-book containing such hymns as that
with which Wesley's collection opens: 'O for a thousand

tongues to sing My great Redeemer's praise!' and 'Leader of
faithful souls, and Guide Of all that travel to the sky', and
'Come, O Thou Traveller unknown,' and 'O Love divine, how
sweet Thou art!'—all by Charles Wesley, and scores of others
almost as good, as well as the great translations by his brother
John: 'Now, I have found the ground wherein Sure my soul's
anchor may remain,' and 'Thee will I love, my strength, my
tower; Thee will I love, my joy, my crown,' can hardly have
words said of them too strong in praise.

But not even to Charles Wesley was there given the power
of self-criticism. In one section of the book 'For Believers
Fighting', one and the same page contains the noble:

> Soldiers of Christ, arise!
> And put your armour on,

and the utterly grotesque:

> O may Thy powerful word
> Inspire a feeble worm
> To rush into Thy kingdom, Lord,
> And take it as by storm!

One might almost posit, if not as *the* constituent of a good
hymn, yet as an absolutely essential element in a hymn-writer,
a sense of the ludicrous.

To come to modern times, I can only mention in passing the
Preface to *The English Hymnal*, which has exercised an influence
more than any other issued during the present century, and
fairly deserves the description, so often misapplied, *epoch-making*. It was extremely well edited. The text of the hymns—
which in its chief rival, *Hymns Ancient and Modern*, was often
scandalously corrupt—(did not some one once say that H. A.
& M. meant 'Hymns asked for and mutilated'?) was restored in
most cases to the original. Above all, the Musical Editor, Dr
Ralph Vaughan Williams, is a man of genius, and, alike in his
own tunes and in those he selected, is able to express the new
musical feeling which the twentieth century has brought.

But *The English Hymnal* itself is deep in debt to another

collection, small in size—only one hundred hymns—but with a
very definite conception of what a hymn ought to be: *The Yattendon Hymnal*, edited, and in great part written, by the late
Poet-Laureate, Dr Robert Bridges. This is not the time nor the
place to attempt an estimate of the place of Dr Bridges in
English literature, or of the influence his work is likely to exercise on the poetry of the future. Now that his austere and
intimidating personality is no longer with us, such an estimate
is perhaps not likely to be so decided as it was when *The Testament of Beauty* was first given to the world. But in hymn-writing,
as in everything else, Dr Bridges had a perfectly definite idea
of what he wished to do, and a haughty intolerance of opinions
and standards and methods other than his own. For several
years he lived at the Berkshire village of Yattendon. Canon
Beeching was rector, and Dr Bridges, in his capacity of precentor, took charge of the music in church, and carried out his
ideas with a ruthlessness which, I gather, was not always appre-
ciated by his fellow-parishioners. No other body of human
beings is quite so conservative as an English country choir, and
we can well imagine the hardly restrained fury of the Yattendon choristers on being confronted at a Christmas service with,
not the familiar hymn and tune that all could sing with their
eyes shut, but

Hark! how all the welkin rings—

no doubt the proper form, as Charles Wesley wrote it—set to
a brand-new tune of repellent dryness by an eminent musician
and friend of their precentor, who thus, in a manner, added
insult to injury.

But Dr Bridges had all a crusader's enthusiasm, and in a
series of papers and letters republished since his death, he
preached his doctrines with characteristic pungency and force.
In one of these papers he emphasizes the 'contrast between the
primitiv Church with its few simple melodies that ravisht the
educated hearer, and our own full-blown institution with its
hymn-book of some six hundred tunes, which, when it is
open'd, fills the sensitiv worshipper'—R. B., we may suppose—
'with dismay, so that ther are persons who would rather not go

inside a church than subject themselves to the trial.' Again:
'It seems to me that the clergy are the responsible people. If
they say that the hymns (words and music) which keep me
away from church draw others thither, and excite useful religious emotions, then they must take the responsibility wholly
on themselves. I would not choose for them. All I can urge is,
that they should hav at least *one* service a week where people
like myself can attend without being offended or moved to
laughter.' Elsewhere he speaks of 'thatt most depressing of all
books ever compiled by the groaning creatur, *Julian's Dictionary* . . . the thousands of carefully tabulated English hymns,
by far the greater number of them not only pitiable as efforts
of human intelligence, but absolutely worthless as vocal
material for melodic treatment.'

It cannot be denied that all this is most offensive—the Oxford don at his very worst—and only partially true. There
were a great many things in hymns, and in the experience
behind hymns, which Bridges did not know, and indeed which
his whole attitude of mind and outlook absolutely shut him out
from knowing. There is, however, another side to him, and
though the quotation I shall now make refers more especially
to music, it brings us very close to what are the constituents of
a good hymn: 'If we consider and ask ourselves what sort of
music we should wish to hear on entering a church, we should
surely, in describing our ideal, say, first of all, that it must be
something different from what is heard elsewhere: that it
should be a sacred music, devoted to its purpos, a music whose
peace should still passion, whose dignity should strengthen our
faith, whose unquestion'd beauty should find a home in our
hearts, to cheer us in life and death; a music worthy of the fair
temples in which we meet, and of the holy words of our liturgy,
a music whose expression of the mystery of things unseen never
allow'd any trifling motiv to ruffle the sanctity of its reserve.
What power for good such a music would hav!'

This is very truly and beautifully said, and the best of the
hymns in *The Yattendon Hymnal* have a lonely and austere
beauty approaching grandeur, whether it be a translation—
and with Bridges the word *translation* is used in the very widest

sense of the term, the original serving mainly, sometimes only,
as the suggestion for a new hymn—or an original poem such as:

> Enter Thy courts, Thou Word of life,
> 　My joy and peace;
> Let the glad sound therein be heard,
> 　Bid plaintive sadness cease.
> Comfort my heart, thou Truth most fair;
> 　O enter in.
> Chasing despair and earth-born care,
> 　My woe and slothful sin.
>
> Glad was the time when I would sing
> 　Thy heavenly praise;
> Happy my heart when Thou wert nigh,
> 　Directing all my ways.
> O let Thy light, Thy joy again
> 　Return to me;
> Nor in disdain from me refrain
> 　Who lift my soul to Thee.
>
> In heav'n and earth Thy law endures,
> 　Thy Word abides;
> My troubled flesh trembleth in awe,
> 　My heart in terror hides.
> Yet still on Thee my heart is set;
> 　In Thee, O Lord,
> I will await, and not forget
> 　The promise of Thy Word.

The Yattendon Hymnal, however great its influence, had a
comparatively limited circulation. Whether one agreed with
its Editor or not in his judgements of inclusion and exclusion,
one could not but acknowledge the very high ideal and the
rigid standard he held before him.

Songs of Praise makes another kind of appeal. In contrast to
the cumbrous format and archaic type of the Yattendon book,
it is both handy and exceedingly cheap. Alike in words and in
music, it has spread its net very widely. In what other collection will you find a sonnet of Shakespeare's, another of Spen-

ser's, part of Wordsworth's 'Ode to Duty', an extract from Shelley's 'Hellas':

> The world's great age begins anew
> The golden years return—

another excerpt from Matthew Arnold's 'Rugby Chapel', yet another from Browning's 'Johannes Agricola in Meditation', Emily Brontë's unforgettable

> No coward soul is mine;
> No trembler in the world's storm-troubled sphere;

and part of a chorus from Hardy's *The Dynasts*, along with the somewhat uncouth and contorted verses of Donald Hankey and Geoffrey Studdert-Kennedy? The practical use of these pieces as hymns may be gauged by the fact that the music to which they are set is, for the most part, extremely difficult to sing.

It is not surprising that a collection so far off the conventional lines was, at its first appearance, met with a storm of criticism. One writer in *The Church Quarterly Review* (April 1930) expressed himself thus: 'It is not superfluous to inform a slipshod age and the compilers of modern high-brow hymn-books that a lyric is that which is suited to be sung, and that metrical meditations by eminent agnostics do not qualify as Songs of Praise!'

Unfortunately, the very clever Editor, Dr Percy Dearmer, did not confine himself to valiant attempts towards raising the literary standard, and widening the scope of our ideas of what a hymn ought to be. '*Songs of Praise*', said the Preface to the original edition (1925), 'is intended to be national, in the sense of including a full expression of that faith which is common to the English-speaking people to-day. . . Some courage in omission will indeed be a necessary part of the religious recovery for which the Churches look . . . and the bad must go, in order that the good may be added.' In pursuance of such an idea, Dr Dearmer did not hesitate to cut and carve and even re-write many of the older hymns, no matter how well known, in order to bring them up to the standard of the doctrine or the religious experience which he himself had reached for the time being, in that most interesting Odyssey of his own. Perhaps the best known example of this unfortunate tendency is his recension of Valiant-for-Truth's song in *The Pilgrim's Progress*.

> Who would true valour see,
> Let him come hither;
> One here will constant be,
> Come wind, come weather—

which, with all its thrill and Shakespearean quality diluted, appears as:

> He who would valiant be
> 'Gainst all disaster,
> Let him in constancy
> Follow the Master.

Dr Dearmer also, unhappily, flooded the book with all sorts of material of widely varying quality. There are twenty-three hymns under his own name, and he disguises his authorship of at least half as many more under a bewildering variety of initials. Dr C. S. Phillips, in his *Hymnody Past and Present*—a most excellent book—has, not at all unkindly, expressed what most people will feel: 'Dr Dearmer . . . like other hymnal compilers before him, does not seem to have been always sufficiently on his guard against the very human prejudice of an author in favour of his own work.' It may also be added that while extremely free in his criticism of other people in *Songs of Praise Discussed*, Dr Dearmer showed himself sensitive to a degree about any criticism passed upon himself and his work, forgetful of the good old adage that 'people who play at bowls must expect rubbers'.

It may safely be predicted that, when a new edition of *Songs of Praise* is called for—and in many respects, more especially on the musical side, it is a very fine collection indeed—the greater part of this editorial deadwood will be cut away. The Church as a whole has every reason to acknowledge with gratitude the service Canon Dearmer rendered by the fertility of his ideas, and the vivacious and challenging manner in which he championed them. He has compelled all writers and users of hymns, as well as compilers of hymn-books, to re-examine their conceptions of the essential constituents of a good hymn—if only by way of contrast to the many bad hymns for which he was himself responsible.

The question may be asked: What are the constituents of a good translation? In the Preface to his *Treasury of Sacred Song*, Palgrave says, 'Translations, as even when at the best (by a law of nature, may I not call it?) hardly ever reaching excellence as poetry, or reaching it only for a moment, are here excluded.' But how much poorer would every hymn-book be if such a self-denying ordinance were passed—and kept—by its compilers! In fact, we can scarcely imagine any hymn-book in which, among the names of authors, those of J. M. Neale, Edward Caswall, Catherine Winkworth, and Jane Borthwick are not to be found.

Translations must be judged, first, by their own merit: what they are in themselves; and secondly, by their faithfulness as renderings of the original.

It is said that Oliver Wendell Holmes and Emerson both agreed that the greatest hymn in the English language was John Wesley's

> Thou hidden love of God, whose height,
> Whose depth unfathom'd, no man knows.

It is, of course, a translation of a hymn by Tersteegen, and in every one of our often-repeated essential constituents—simplicity, sincerity, fervour, imagination, etc.—it far surpasses the original. Here certainly John Wesley's powers are seen at their height. I cannot altogether agree with the opinion recently expressed, that his 'sense of fitness in style was unerring. His alterations of other writers' hymns, such as Watts's superb "Before Jehovah's awful throne", were always marked improvements.' I recall the disastrous failure of his attempt to re-write George Herbert's exquisite:

> Teach me, my God and King,
> In all things Thee to see.

But confront him with some hymn by Tersteegen, Zinzendorf, Rothe, or Gerhardt, perhaps not specially distinguished in itself, and straightway his lips are touched as by a live coal from the altar. All his powers are awake. His imagination takes wings. He forgets to argue, and never ceases to wonder and adore.

> Now I have found the ground wherein
>   Sure my soul's anchor may remain—
> The wounds of Jesus, for my sin
>   Before the world's foundation slain;
> Whose mercy shall unshaken stay
> When heaven and earth shall flee away.

Two other translators I would mention. The first is Isaac Williams, whose hymn for the Feast of Apostles and Evangelists is all that a translation should be for clean-cut masculine vigour:

> Disposer Supreme, and Judge of the earth,
>   Who choosest for Thine, the weak and the poor;
> To frail earthen vessels and things of no worth,
>   Intrusting Thy riches which aye shall endure;
>
> Their sound goeth forth, Christ Jesus is Lord!
>   Then Satan doth fear, his citadels fall:
> As when the dread trumpets went forth at Thy word,
>   And one long blast shattered the Canaanites' wall.

The second is Miss Helen Waddell, perhaps the greatest of living translators of Medieval Latin Verse; her touch at its best is little short of magical. Most of us know Neale's translation of Abelard's

> *O quanta qualia sunt illa sabbata,*
> O what their joy and their glory must be—

the hymn which Canon Liddon used to give out in St Paul's whenever he had the opportunity. Here is part of Miss Waddell's rendering—would that she had essayed the metre of the original!

How mighty are the Sabbaths,
  How mighty and how deep,
That the high courts of heaven
  To everlasting keep,
What peace unto the weary,
  What pride unto the strong,
When God in Whom are all things
  Shall be all things to men! . . .

Jerusalem is the city
  Of everlasting peace,
A peace that is surpassing
  And utter blessedness;
Where finds the dreamer waking,
  Truth beyond dreaming far,
Nor there the heart's possessing
  Less than the heart's desire. . .

There all vexation ended,
  And from all grieving free,
We sing the Song of Zion
  In deep security.
And everlasting praises
  For all Thy gifts of grace
Rise from Thy happy people,
  Lord of our blessedness!

One thing more must be touched upon in closing. It may be paradoxical to put it in such a manner, but it is emphatically true, that *the most important constituent of a good hymn is a good tune to which it may be sung.* No hymn ever soars—at best it trails only a broken wing—unless you find it difficult to read it without the tune singing itself in your head all the time. You cannot judge a hymn-tune by purely musical standards alone, any more than you can or ought to settle the quality and usefulness of a hymn by those which are purely literary. Within certain limits the same qualities *must be looked for* in *tunes* as in *hymns*, and what *these* are may be discovered by the method of examining tunes which are confessedly in the front rank.

First, *Something to Say*: that is, a real singable melody, with strength and progress and climax in it, not a mere dull succession of notes, however venerable its tradition may be, or however eminent its composer. Then, as *positive* qualities: sincerity, simplicity, dignity, fervour, imagination; and *negatively*, the absence of anything merely conventional, sentimental, or sophisticated. When the first thing you think or say of a tune, as of a hymn, is 'How clever!' you may be almost certain that it is bad.

When all is said and done, in trying to discover what really are the constituents of a good hymn, we come back to the words of that Preface to the *Collection of Hymns for use of the People called Methodists*, dated 20 October 1779, part of which has been quoted already: A good hymn is that which serves in any man as 'a means of raising or quickening the spirit of devotion, of confirming his faith; of enlivening his hope; and of kindling and increasing his love to God and man. When Poetry thus keeps its place as the hand-maid of Piety, it shall attain, not a poor, perishable wreath, but a crown that fadeth not away.'

JUPITER CARLYLE AND THE SCOTTISH
MODERATES

THE history of Moderatism in Scotland in the eighteenth century has never been written with the fullness which such a movement—if that name be appropriate to what was essentially static—most certainly deserves. The relevant literature—both contemporary and later—is abundant. In the eighteenth century people had a positive rage for self-expression, in diaries, autobiographies, sermons, pamphlets, poems; one wonders how the comparatively primitive printing-presses of the day were able to cope with the demands of writers and readers alike. Much of what was published was of course ephemeral, and is now utterly dead. But a book like Dr Alexander Carlyle's *Autobiography* is as living in its own way as anything in Burns or Boswell. Of the Moderates themselves there have been studies and monographs; in a past generation Dean Stanley's Lectures and Dr Rainy's Reply; more recently those by Henry Grey Graham,[1] and Dr John Watson,[2] and Dr Joseph Leckie[3]; but, so far as I know, there has been nothing co-ordinating the mass of detail, and giving a general survey. Such a study of the whole field is one of the chief *desiderata* in Scottish Church History.

As we pass in the history of Scotland from the seventeenth to the eighteenth century we are at once conscious of a change: there is a ˙certain slackening of the pulse, a lowering of the temperature. The reason lies in the transition made at the turn of the century from a heroic age to the Age of Reason.

In the one period we have picturesque figures like the two great Marquises, Montrose and Argyll, and churchmen like Henderson and Rutherford, to be succeeded by the Covenanters and Martyrs—Peden, Cameron and Renwick, John Brown of Priesthill and Donald Cargill, Grisel Hume and Margaret Wilson; these on the one side, and on the other such formidable personalities as Claverhouse, Dalzell, Lauderdale,

---

[1] *Social Life in Scotland in the Eighteenth Century.*
[2] *The Eighteenth Century Scot.*
[3] *Secession Worthies.*

Mackenzie, and Sharp. There are in our public galleries and engraved in countless books portraits of many of these, so that if they were to present themselves before us, we would recognize them at once.

But comparatively few know the outward appearance of Carstares (he is actually represented with a beard on a carved pulpit in Dunblane Cathedral!) or of Thomas Boston, or of John Duke of Argyll and Greenwich (Jeanie Deans's Duke), or of Fletcher of Saltoun. This may partly be owing to the fashions of that time—above all, to the flowing periwig which standardizes everybody's appearance and at first sight makes it difficult to distinguish, say, Dean Swift from Bishop Butler! There is more than this mere resemblance on the surface, whether of men or things.

The beginning of the eighteenth century in Scotland saw a nation that was tired, indisposed for anything adventurous either in Church or State, glad to have at long last the opportunity of living quietly, and grateful to a government that provided the protection that was necessary. Life under a Stuart régime might be interesting and colourful; it provided, as we know, opportunities for the exercise of the noblest heroism among gentle and simple alike. But the dynasty had become an unmitigated nuisance to the majority of decent people in the country, and, by the time the seventeenth century had yet a dozen years to run, it had become emphatically like 'that which decayeth and waxeth old, and is ready to vanish away.'

The Scottish nation had been hard hit, alike in pride and in purse, by the disasters of the Darien Expedition, and it remained sullenly suspicious of the manœuvrings which culminated in the legislative and Parliamentary Union with England in 1707. It is not easy for us nowadays to understand why a movement which in the long run—and not so very long, after all—proved to be of unquestionable advantage to both nations, was in Scotland at the time so bitterly resisted and resented. This was not due merely to a sentimental feeling at what Chancellor Seafield called 'the end of an auld sang'. Mr R. L. Mackie's words represent truly enough the general attitude of Scotland: 'The crown, the sceptre, the sword of State were borne out, to be lost for a hundred years: the Commissioner, the scarlet-robed peers, the lairds and burgesses filed for the last time under the tapestried walls and through the great doorway, to the cowed and sullen crowds without. *Te Deums* might be sung in St Paul's, the guns of the Tower might thunder the news to a rejoicing London, but many a Scotsman felt that day that his country had received a mortal wound.'[1]

'Weary on Lunnon, and a' that e'er came out o't!' says Miss Grizel Damahoy, an aged seamstress, in *The Heart of Midlothian*[2]; 'they hae taen away our parliament and they hae oppressed our trade. Our gentles will hardly allow that a Scots needle can sew ruffles on a sark, or lace on an owerlay.' 'Ye may say that, Miss Damahoy, and I ken o' them that hae gotten raisins frae Lunnon by forpits at ance,' responded Plumdamas; 'and then sic an host of idle English gaugers and excisemen as hae come down to vex and torment us, that an honest man canna fetch sae muckle as a bit anker o' brandy frae Leith to the Lawnmarket, but he's like to be robbit o' the very gudes he's bought and paid for.'

The whole country was depressed. Not yet had the West Indian trade brought prosperity to the Clyde. Many years were to pass before Edinburgh rose to the peak of its intellectual glory, when its *literati* were the arbiters in taste and philosophy to the half of Europe; when professors like McLaurin and the Gregories attracted students from the Continent, and Raeburn's men and women in all the pride of their exuberant vitality were to be seen walking about its streets.

It is as such things are remembered that it is possible to understand how *Moderatism* came to have its hold in Scotland, changing its policy, and tightening its grip as the social and commercial and political life of the people altered, and the *praefervidum ingenium Scotorum* began, with the new conditions, to take new form and colour.

The Revolution Settlement under King William and Carstares gave to the Church of Scotland a place and a security—so far as outward conditions went—such as it had not known

[1] *History of Scotland*, p. 472.
[2] Chapter iv.

G

since the Reformation. But the State demanded its *quid pro quo*. An Act restoring lay patronage, which had been abolished in 1690, was, largely under Jacobite influence, pushed through Parliament in 1712, and remained a root of bitterness in Scotland till its happy disappearance in 1874. But other forces much more subtle and disintegrating than any merely external pressure, were at work within the Church itself, weakening its ancient testimony; and they were the more formidable because they corresponded to what was being thought and said all over Western Europe at that time and had in them a real element of truth, hitherto largely obscured.

The whole outlook of the nation was changing. Professor Hume Brown says:[1]

'From the Reformation to the Revolution religion was the dominant factor in the determination of public policy. . . It was religion that had dethroned Mary and Charles I and James VII, and these successive events mark the turning-points in the national destinies throughout the entire period. But from the Revolution onwards . . . religion no longer constitutes the warp and woof of the story of the Scottish people, and becomes but one of the diverse strands of which the entire web is composed. Trade, commerce, industry, literature, and developing thought become concurrent factors with it in the growth of national life; and, like these various interests, it is but one other phase of the national mind.'

This very interesting generalization was written in 1911, but, however true it may be of the present day, I venture to question its truth of the period about which it was written. Again and again in all sorts of histories of Scotland in the eighteenth century it is asserted that the Secession of 1733 was made on account of Patronage; but the Secession Fathers themselves always declared this to be quite a secondary issue. I distinctly recall a very old lady, a daughter of the Secession Manse, steeped in the traditions of the Secession, saying—I am afraid with a side glance at Free Church contendings—'It wasn't Patronage we came out on. It was doctrine.' The Moderates themselves made no mistake on this point. Dr Somerville,

---

[1] History of Scotland, iii, 232-3.

Minister of Jedburgh, gives an account[1] of an interview he had
with Charles James Fox during a visit to London in 1791.

'He gave me a frank reception, and in the course of our conversation introduced pertinent questions relative to the constitution of the Church of Scotland and the business in agita-
tion (i.e. the proposed extension by Government of the Test
Act of Charles II to members of the Church of Scotland). One
of these questions was, Who are the people whom you call
Seceders in Scotland—what are their discriminating tenets?
I suppose they are of the same temper with the party in England called *Low Churchmen*, and you of the Establishment be-
long to *the High Church Party*. I answered, Quite the reverse.
The Scotch Seceders are the High Church Party, for they con-
tend for maintaining the doctrines and discipline of the Kirk
in all the strictness, and to all the extent established and practised in Scotland according to the Directory of the Assembly
of Divines in 1648; and I added that, with his permission, I
would furnish him with such documents as would contain an
answer to his question in more explicit terms than I could employ. I called again in a few days with a copy of the *Act and
Testimony* 1736, and also some of the Fast Day Sermons and
tracts published at that time by the Ministers who began the
Secession, and were deemed the oracles of the Sect, marking
with the pencil the sentences which I wished him to notice, and
I remember that he seemed to be much amused, and smiled
while reading them. The passage which amused him the most
was a description of the predominant national sins, and the
judgements impending over the nation on that account; and
among the former the discontinuing prosecution for witchcraft
was expressly specified.'

Surely the Comic Muse never devised anything more after her
own heart than Charles James Fox fresh from a night at the
gaming tables at Brooks's wrestling with the *Secession Testimony*! But there is no doubt that good Dr Somerville was absolutely right in his diagnosis of the situation, though the early
Seceders were concerned with much more important issues
than witch-finding or even the obligation to keep up the

---

[1] *My Life and Times* (pp. 234-6), a book indispensable to those who
would form a just idea of what was best in the Church at this time.

annual signing of the Covenants at the Summer Sacrament.
This could not be better put than in a well-known passage in
Thomas Carlyle's *Reminiscences*, in which he speaks of the
'Burgher' Kirk at Ecclefechan in which he was brought up:

'All Dissent in Scotland is mainly a stricter adherence to the
National Kirk in all points, and the then Dissenterage is de-
finable to moderns simply as a Free Kirk making no noise. It
had quietly, about 1740, after much haggle and remonstrance,
seceded or walked out of its stipends, officialities, and dignities,
greatly to the mute sorrow of religious Scotland, and was still
in a strict manner on united Voluntary principles preaching to
the people what of best and sacredest it could. Except on stated
occasions . . . there was little, almost no talk, especially no
preaching at all, about patronage or secular control, but all
turned on the weightier and universal matters of the law, and
was considerably entitled to say for itself, *Hear, all men*.'[1]

At the same time Dr Hume Brown is correct in emphasizing
the influence of the *Aufklärung* as felt in Scotland in the growing spirit of Scepticism, and the desire to make Reason alike
the foundation and the touch-stone of everything. It was
against *this* that 'Hill men' and 'Marrow men' alike fought; it
was *this* that underlay the Simson Controversy, this that supplied not only all the theology that the Moderates ever possessed, but the greater part of their background and atmosphere. A recent apologist[2] for the Moderates, in a popular
text-book, categorically denies that they were not true to the
Christian faith; and it may be freely admitted that the Moderates did not attack the faith like Voltaire, or undermine its
foundations like Hume. Theirs was rather a certain bluntness
of perception, an inability to grasp what the real issue is, a
kind of puzzled astonishment that sensible people should make
so much work about it. Now we must avoid what Bishop
Butler has called 'the giving of characters'.[3] We can no more
sum up against an ecclesiastical party than bring an indictment
against a whole nation. It is rather by *what it left out*, whether

[1] Carlyle, *Reminiscences*, ii: Edward Irving.
[2] Dr A. J. Campbell.
[3] Sermon on The Government of the Tongue.

deliberately or from sheer ignorance, that moderate *preaching*
—I doubt very much if it ever had much of a *theology*—is to be
judged.

One thing the Moderates did which has left its mark on the
religious and devotional life of the Scottish Church. They were
responsible for the Collection, *Translations and Paraphrases in
Verse of several Passages of Sacred Scripture.*[1]

On the value of the Paraphrases as a whole many diverse
opinions have been held and expressed. Mr J. Hepburn Mil-
lar[2] has given what might be taken to be the typical 'Moderate'
estimate, with a full-blooded vigour which leaves nothing to be
desired:

'The Paraphrases form incomparably the best collection of
Sacred Lyrics (or 'Gospel Sonnets') for its size which has ever
been made in the English Language. Devout, dignified, and
reticent, they afford a truly admirable medium for expressing
the religious feelings and aspirations of an intelligent, educated,
and self-respecting people. Their genuine piety is untainted by
extravagance, their grave serenity unruffled by hysteria. They
that seek for glitter, banality, and noise, must turn to the more
comprehensive volumes of a later date, whence they will not be
sent empty away. It is one of the most significant symptoms of
the degeneration which, as some believe, is overtaking the
Scottish character, that this excellent little collection is falling
into something like desuetude in public worship.'

This is truly to

> Gar oor streams and burnies shine
> Up wi' the best.

On the other hand, like practically every other collection,

---

[1] The history of this is extremely complicated, and any student of the
subject cannot do better than consult what is really the last word on it,
Mr Douglas J. Maclagan's *The Scottish Paraphrases*, in which the whole story
of the Collection, the names and biographies of those who were engaged in
the work, the sources from which they drew, the methods they used, the
different versions which they issued before the final form in 1781, are all
treated with a careful research that exhausts the subject, and a scholarship
that is beyond all praise.

[2] *Literary History of Scotland*, p. 379.

larger or smaller, it *dates*. As a whole it could hardly have been
made at any other time but the eighteenth century; and though
in many respects a century which contains such names as
Watts and Doddridge, Cowper and Newton, and, above all,
Charles and John Wesley, could hardly be called anything but
a Golden Age in British Hymnody,[1] still a great part of it—its
thought and mode of expression—is as dead as it could well be;
and the world in which we live is as different as could be
imagined from that of those spacious and leisurely days. Of the
sixty-seven Paraphrases, twenty-five at least are never—and
never could be—sung. Of the remaining forty-two, perhaps a
score could be used, for the most part, in judiciously made
extracts; yet even these would sound somewhat strangely
except in Scotland and in places where the exiled Scot meets
his brother to worship God after the fashion of their fathers.
But the very best of the Paraphrases, 'O God of Bethel', 'Come,
let us to the Lord our God', 'Where high the heavenly temple
stands', ''Twas on that night', 'I'm not ashamed to own my
Lord', 'Father of Peace and God of Love', 'How bright these
glorious spirits shine'—to take seven, of which three are by
Scotsmen, can hold up their heads in any company.

But now, let us turn from history strictly so-called, to biography, and see how the principles on which Moderatism
rested worked themselves out in a very typical Scot, Alexander
Carlyle, for fifty-seven years Minister at Inveresk in the shire of
East Lothian.

First of all, let me give three estimates of Carlyle, none the
less interesting by their being given off-hand, by three very
different men:

(1) 'The grandest demi-god I ever saw was Dr Carlyle, minis-
      ter of Musselburgh, and a shrewd, clever old carle he was,
      no doubt, but no more a poet than his precentor.'

(2) 'The Rev. Dr Carlyle must have had some substantial
      merit, for he was the associate of all the most eminent men
      of his time, and is respectfully mentioned in most of their

[1] George Sampson calls it 'The Century of Divine Songs' (Warton
Lecture).

biographies, and he was one of the noblest-looking old gentlemen I almost ever beheld.'

(3) 'That pot-walloping Sadducee, Jupiter Carlyle.'

The man on whom such diverse and characteristic verdicts were pronounced by judges so eminent as Sir Walter Scott, Lord Cockburn, and Thomas Carlyle, must have been worth knowing. Cockburn's estimate seems to show that even in the generation immediately after his own, Alexander Carlyle had already become something of a mystery—one of those men who, in Church and State, wield a great influence, no one can exactly tell why. The mystery was partly, though not entirely, revealed more than half a century after his death. It had long been known that in his later years Dr Carlyle had been engaged on an autobiography, and those who had been privileged to read the unfinished MS. spoke with the warmest appreciation of its merits. In 1860 the book, skilfully edited by John Hill Burton, book-hunter and historian, appeared. At once it took its place as one of the half-dozen books absolutely indispensable to all who wish to understand eighteenth-century Scotland, as casting a most curious light, not only on the character of its writer and his associates, but on the type of thought and religion prevailing in his day.

Born on 26 January 1722, in the Manse of Cummertrees, Dumfriesshire, where his father was minister before removing to Prestonpans two years later, studying at the Universities of Edinburgh, Glasgow, and Leyden, settled at Inveresk in 1748, and living there for fifty-seven years till his death on 25 August 1805 at the age of eighty-three, Carlyle 'dwelt among his own people' from first to last. But he was anything but parochial in his outlook. He had an uncommonly quick eye, a most tenacious memory, a 'Herodotean relish for a racy anecdote', and an absolutely unsparing causticity of language. Consequently the *Autobiography*, although it was not begun till the writer's seventy-eighth birthday, has a vigour and vivacity of style which carry the reader on with unflagging interest from the first page to the last. Would that he had set himself to his task earlier! The book breaks off abruptly at the year 1770 when

the author was in the full vigour of his prime, leaving his story
no more than half told. Only three years afterwards, Dr Johnson
lumbered into Edinburgh on his famous journey to the Hebrides;
and, thirteen years later still, in 1786, Robert Burns flashed like
a portent across the sky of the city before its amazed if patron-
izing *literati*. Whether Carlyle actually met either Johnson or
Burns is not known, but he was in the closest touch with those
who did. One would give much for his comments on both men,
as extraordinarily different from himself, as they were from
each other.

The Scotland of five generations ago was a country very
unlike that known to us. 'The New Road', as Neil Munro calls
it in his story with that title, had begun to open up the hitherto
almost trackless north. But, so far as means of communication
went, the Lowlands were little, if at all, more accessible than
the Highlands, to the traveller. When Carlyle set out on any of
his frequent journeys to Newcastle or London, it was always on
horseback that he took his leisurely way. The view to-day
from the knoll on which Inveresk Church stands—a church
which he built, but never preached in, as it was not opened
until a couple of weeks after his death—is as pleasant as eye
could desire, over hill and vale and farm and thriving country
towns and villages, away to the Lammermuirs, the Pentlands,
and Arthur's Seat, and round to the gleaming Firth of Forth,

A land made blithe with plough and harrow.

But in mid-eighteenth century the landscape was naked and
treeless; the fields were unenclosed, the soil was undrained and
sour with stagnant pools in the marshy levels—a principal
cause of the ague which almost till within living memory swept
like a plague throughout Lowland farm-towns every spring;
and the houses were comfortless and insanitary to the last
degree. It would be a complete mistake, however, to imagine
that the people living amid such untoward conditions must
have been like slum-dwellers to-day. The average rate of
intelligence was high, and though the range of reading and
thought might in our own day be considered narrow enough,
interest was keen in the deepest things of life. The schools and

schoolmasters John Knox set up had not laboured in vain.

Carlyle entered the University of Edinburgh at the preposterously early age of thirteen, and studied mathematics under the famous Colin McLaurin, whose epitaph in sonorous Latin may be seen high on the outside of the south wall of Greyfriars Church. He naïvely tells us that his class-work cost him little trouble, his father having carried him through the first book of Euclid in the previous summer!

There is a refreshing pungency in his remarks on his professors. 'There was one advantage attending the lectures of a dull professor—viz. that he could form no school, and the students were left entirely to themselves and naturally formed opinions far more liberal than those they got from the Professor.'

Much more exciting than any class lectures was the escape of the smuggler, George Robertson, during a service in the Tolbooth Church, and the execution of his companion, Andrew Wilson, in the Grassmarket. It gives one a certain *grue* to read that Carlyle's tutor, for the benefit of his pupils, had taken a window 'where we went in due time to see the show.' To this, Carlyle has the grace to add, 'I had no small aversion.'

This led, as we know, in the following autumn to the famous 'Porteous Mob', of which even Scott's description in *The Heart of Midlothian* is not more vivid than Carlyle's.

His College course continued on its ordered way, interspersed by long summer vacations, spent for the most part with relatives in the country.

At the age of twenty-one Carlyle migrated to Glasgow, in order to complete his Divinity course at the University there. It was the Glasgow of Bailie Nicol Jarvie; a pleasant town with a Green worthy of the name, a college embosomed in shady alleys and flower gardens, and a river which could easily be waded at a still golden 'Broomielaw'. Comparing the two Universities, Carlyle remarks that 'although at that time there appeared to be a marked superiority in the best scholars and most diligent students of Edinburgh, yet in Glasgow, learning seemed to be an object of more importance, and the habit of application was much more general.'

The chief stars in the Academical Galaxy of the West at that time were William Leechman, professor of Divinity, Francis Hutcheson, a pioneer of the Scottish Philosophy, and Robert Simson, the eminent mathematician whose edition of Euclid held the field almost to our own day. Of all these Carlyle gives amusing sketches, which serve to emphasize the extraordinary change that has passed over the customs and ideals of academic life since the days immediately before the '45. Students took their duties as easily as did their professors. There was little sport in the modern sense, though Carlyle, as became a man brought up within easy reach of Musselburgh Links, was an excellent golfer, greatly astonishing at a later time his English friends, David Garrick among them, by his prowess with club and ball. Debating Societies, meeting in taverns near the University, flourished greatly, and the amount of liquor consumed was, in every sense of the word, staggering.

It was a hard-drinking age, claret and brandy being the beverages most drunk; but one has to read the *Autobiography* to understand the hold that this habit had over society in general. What a light is cast by an off-hand sketch of Dr Patrick Cuming, one of the leaders of the Moderate party: 'Had his temper been equal to his talents he might have kept [his position] long, for he had both learning and sagacity and very agreeable conversation, with a constitution able to bear the conviviality of the times.' By his own testimony Carlyle is convicted of an excess which goes far to justify the opprobrious epithet applied to him by his famous namesake. But even *he* was excelled by Dr Alexander Webster, the leader of the Evangelical party in the Church of Scotland.

'His appearance of great strictness in religion . . . not acting in restraint of his convivial humour, he was held to be excellent company even by those of dissolute manners; while being a five-bottle man, he could lay them all under the table. This had brought on him the nickname of *Dr Bonum Magnum* in the time of faction; but never being indecently the worse of liquor, and a love of claret to any degree not being reckoned in those days a sin in Scotland, all his excesses were pardoned.'

The hopeful young theological student, having now almost

completed his course, with the exception of a term at a foreign
Protestant University, returned to the Manse at Prestonpans,
from which he set out on a series of visits to the members of the
Haddington Presbytery in preparation for his 'licence' as a
full-fledged probationer. In thumb-nail sketches of these, his
caustic humour finds free play. Mr Dickson of Aberlady, 'a
well-bred formal old man, reckoned a good preacher, though
lame enough in the article of knowledge, or indeed in discernment'; Mr James Glen of Dirleton, 'fat and unwieldy, good-
natured and open-hearted, very social though quick-tempered
and jealous'; Mr George Murray of North Berwick, 'a dry,
withered stick . . . very worthy and sensible, though at the age
of fifty as torpid in mind as in body'; Mr John Witherspoon of
Yester—father of the famous President of Princeton—'too lazy
to engage in anything so arduous as the examination of a
student—how to eat and drink and sleep being his sole care,
though he was not without parts, if the soul had not been
buried under a mountain of flesh'; Mr Lundie of Saltoun, 'a
pious and primitive old man, very respectful in his manners
and very kind'; Mr Matthew Simson of Pencaitland, 'an excellent examinator, for he answered all his own questions': we
see them all; and can only wonder what *they* thought of this
formidable son of their quiet neighbour at Prestonpans.

Trials of a very different kind than those appointed by a
Presbytery for would-be licentiates were soon to come, not
only to Carlyle but to the whole country. As the song has it,

> The news frae Moidart cam' yestreen
> Will sune gar many ferlie.

Prince Charlie raised his standard at Glenfinnan on 19
August 1745, and about a month later—none too soon—the
Edinburgh citizens, young Carlyle among them, were forming
themselves into volunteer corps, and drilling in the manual
exercise.

'The mob in the street and the ladies in the windows treated
us very variously, many with lamentations and even with tears,
and some with apparent scorn and derision. In one house there
was a row of windows full of ladies, who appeared to enjoy our
march to danger with much levity and mirth. Some of our

warm Volunteers observed them, and threatened to fire into the windows if they were not instantly let down, which was immediately complied with. In marching down the Bow, . . . the scene was different, for all the spectators were in tears, and uttering loud lamentations. . . Principal Wishart called upon us in a most pathetic speech to desist from this rash enterprise, which, he said, was exposing the flower of the Youth of Edinburgh and the hope of the next generation to the danger of being cut off, or made prisoners, and maltreated without any just or adequate object . . . and therefore he prayed and besought the Volunteers and their officers to give up all thoughts of leaving the city defenceless, to be a prey to the seditious.'

Such being the temper of the degenerate successors of Knox and Buchanan, with magistrates not one whit more courageous, there is little wonder that the city opened its gates to the Prince without striking a blow.

The Battle of Prestonpans followed in a few days, and Carlyle, who had walked home shortly before Lochiel's Highlanders entered Edinburgh, has left an extraordinarily vivid account of that confused engagement, which he saw from the manse garden. 'This view I had of the rebel army confirmed me in the prepossession that nothing but the weakest and most unaccountable bad conduct on our part could have possibly given them victory.'

From the first, however, he and other shrewd judges had little doubt of the ultimate result.

'The court at the Abbey was dull and sombre—the Prince was melancholy; he seemed to have no confidence in anybody, not even in the ladies who were much his friends; far less had he the spirit to venture to the High Church of Edinburgh and take the Sacrament, as his great-uncle Charles II had done the Covenant, which would have secured him the low-country Commons. . . He had not a mind fit for command at any time, far less to rule the Highland chiefs in prosperity. . . I had the good fortune to see him, as I was close by him when he walked through the guard. He was a good-looking man of about five feet ten inches; his hair was dark red, and his eyes black. His features were regular, his visage long, much sunburnt and freckled, and his countenance thoughtful and melancholy.'

This is not at all the 'Bonnie Prince Charlie' of popular legend, the 'Young Chevalier' of *Waverley* and the Jacobite Songs; but the description is probably near enough the truth, and it helps us to understand the fiasco of the '45, and the lamentable moral and physical break-down of the last tragical years in Rome.

While the Prince was still wasting precious time in Holyrood, Carlyle set out for Holland. It is unnecessary to enter into the details of his stay there, though, as we read the *Autobiography*, we can almost hear the self-appreciative ruminating chuckle with which fifty years afterwards the old man sets down his reminiscences. He took out his four prescribed classes at Leyden, but 'having heard all the professors could say in a much better form at home, we went but rarely, and for form's sake only, to hear the Dutchmen.' All the more time was left on their hands for sight-seeing, for skating on the canals, and, above all, for social life. Carlyle readily made friends with many other students like himself, and with young men completing their education, so called, by doing the 'Grand Tour' of Europe under the nominal care of easy-going and incompetent tutors. Among these was a lad of eighteen with a loose tongue and a horrible squint, who was yet to win great notoriety, John Wilkes, 'whose ugly countenance in early youth was very striking. . . I came to know Wilkes very well afterwards, and found him to be a sprightly entertaining fellow. too much so for his years, for even then he showed something of daring profligacy, for which he was afterwards notorious.'

No report of their diligence in study being required in those easy-going days, Carlyle and his companions spent what was doubtless to them a very agreeable winter, returning to England in the spring of 1746 with little Dutch divinity in their minds, but with a very considerably enlarged stock of experience in the ways of the world.

Home again, Carlyle lost no time in taking licence as a probationer, and preached his first sermon on the Fast Day at Tranent. 'This', he complacently says, 'met with universal approbation. The genteel people of Prestonpans parish were all there; and one young lady to whom I had been long

attached, not having been able to conceal her admiration of
my oratory,'—hark to the fellow!—'I inwardly applauded my
own resolution of adhering to the promise I had made my
family to persevere in the clerical profession.'

In due course he was presented to the parish of Inveresk,
though, he says, 'there arose much murmuring against me as
too young and too much addicted to the company of my
superiors, to be fit for so important a charge, together with
many doubts about my having the Grace of God, an occult
quality which the people cannot define, but surely is in full
opposition to the defects they saw in me.' So began the long
ministry which lasted a little more than fifty-seven years.

In the *Autobiography* itself we do not read much of any
definitely pastoral or other ministerial work. The inscription
on the tombstone against the wall of Inveresk Church describes
him as '||faithful to his pastoral charge||not ambitious of popu-
lar applause||, but to the people a willing guide||in the ways
of righteousness||and truth'||; and beneath the conventional
phraseology we may assume a substratum of fact.

So far as concerns his public life and policy in Church
courts, there never was any doubt about the position of Carlyle and his friends. In opposition to the 'High Flying' party,
as he calls them, led by Dr Alexander Webster—'the *noirest* of
his many *bêtes*', to quote a happy phrase of Professor R. A. S.
Macalister's—he says,

'There were a few of us who, besides the levity of youth and
the natural freedom of our manners, had an express design to
throw contempt on that vile species of hypocrisy which mag-
nified an indecorum into a crime,[1] and gave an air of false

[1] This phrase seems to have pleased Carlyle. In his *Sermon preached at
Edinburgh before the Synod of Lothian*, 5 May 1767, we read: 'Hence the
liberty that is taken of making truth and conscience to be only of one side;
of branding each other with the names of Libertine and Hypocrite; of
magnifying an indecorum into a crime, or of construing a severe or morose
demeanour to be vile grimace; while the enemies of our church lie in wait
for such fair opportunities of seducing the credulous from every side, and
the foes of religion sit *in the scorner's chair and laugh*'. *The Tendency of the Constitution of the Church of Scotland to form the Temper, Spirit, and Character of her
Ministers*, p. 33.

sanctimony and Jesuitism to the greatest part of the clergy, and was thereby pernicious to national religion. In this plan we succeeded, for in the midst of our freedom having preserved respect, and obtained a leading in the Church, we freed the Clergy from many unreasonable and hypocritical restraints.'

The special allusion here is to the part which Carlyle played in the controversy that arose when his friend, the Rev. John Home of Athelstaneford, about the end of 1756, brought out in the Edinburgh Theatre his tragedy of *Douglas*, a work now remembered, if at all, by two lines only:

My name is Norval: On the Grampian Hills
My father feeds his flocks.

It was received with unbounded enthusiasm, one of the audience, so the story goes, rising up in the pit and expressing the feelings of all by shouting, 'Whaur's your Wullie Shakespeare noo?' But the author was a minister, and several of his clerical friends, Carlyle among them, had openly attended the performance, and the scandalized Church Courts took action against Home. Carlyle at once brought out, under the title *An Argument to prove that the Tragedy of Douglas ought to be publicly burnt by the Hands of the Hangman*, a satirical pamphlet which, as he says, 'had a great effect by elating our friends, and perhaps more in exasperating our enemies'. He was summoned before the Presbytery of Dalkeith to answer for his conduct, but stood his ground, and in the end the libel against him was defeated, though the Assembly to which the case had finally been appealed passed an Act declaratory, forbidding the clergy to countenance the theatre. This Act, however, became almost immediately a dead letter, and twenty-eight years afterwards —so he triumphantly records—when Mrs Siddons visited Edinburgh, 'during the sitting of the General Assembly, that court was obliged to fix all its important business for the alternate days when she did not act, as all the younger members, clergy as well as laity, took their stations in the theatre on those days by three in the afternoon.'

This victory gave Carlyle an important place in the counsels of the Moderates, of whom Principal Robertson was leader. He could always be counted upon by his party whether in

intrigue or in open debate, and, by his own frank acknow-
ledgement, he was not at all disposed to be scrupulous in
either. With all his geniality there was a certain callous streak
in him, as the following story shows. At the Assembly of 1766
the Evangelical party had brought in an overture to make an
inquiry into the causes and extent of Schism in the Church
and the most expedient measures for remedying the evil.[1] This
the Moderates determined to oppose with all their strength.

'On Friday 29th May there was a very long debate, so that
the vote was not called till past seven o'clock. Jardine—[Min-
ister of the Tron Church, Dean of the Thistle, and a well-
known leader and oracle of the Moderates]—who had for
some time complained of breathlessness, had seated himself
on a high bench near the east door of the Assembly House,
there being at that time no galleries erected. He had, not half-
an-hour before, had a communication with some ladies near
him in the Church gallery, who had sent him a bottle of wine,
of which he took one glass. The calling of the roll began, and
when it passed the Presbytery of Lochmaben, he gave a significant look with his eye to me who was sitting below the throne, as
much as to say, 'Now the day's our own'. I had turned to the
left to whisper to John Home, who was next me, the sign I had

---

[1] It is interesting to learn the views of Dr Somerville of Jedburgh on
Schism. 'There was a time within my memory when with a very few
exceptions, secession was regarded as in every view teeming with incal-
culable mischief. If the number of individuals who entertain such an
opinion is now diminished, it affords at least a presumptive proof that
experience has not justified these gloomy forebodings. So far from believing
secession and schism to be evils, I am inclined to think that they have been
productive of beneficial effects with respect to the ecclesiastical establishment, as well as to the more important interests of religion. It will not be
denied that the influence of religion upon the great body of the people
must in no small degree depend upon the fidelity, the diligence, and exemplary conduct of its officiating ministers. The first and most obvious effect
of secession is to excite, if I may so express it, a competition for character
between the Established clergy and their Dissenting brethren. The lower
ranks of the people may not be qualified to discern the nicer shades of moral
distinction; they may be deceived by arrogant pretensions, and fallacious
forms of virtue; but they are sufficiently qualified to judge of those depart-
ments of ministerial duty which come under their own observation and

got; before I could look round again, Jardine had tumbled from his seat, and being a man of six feet two inches and of large bones, had borne down all those on the two benches below him, and fallen to the ground. He was immediately carried out to the passage, and the roll-calling stopped. Various reports came from the door, but, anxious to know the truth, I stepped behind the Moderator's chair and over the green table, and with difficulty made the door through a very crowded house. When I came there, I found him lying stretched on the pavement of the passage with many people about him, among the rest his friend and mine, James Russel, the surgeon. With some difficulty I got near him, and whispered was it not a faint? 'No, no,' replied he, 'it is all over.' I returned to the house, and resuming my place, gave out that there were hopes of his recovery. This composed the house, and the calling of the roll went on, when it was carried to reject the overture by a great majority. This was a deadly blow to the enemies of presentations, for they had mustered all their strength, and had been strenuous in debate. . . Robertson was much dejected, as he had good reason. I immediately proposed to him and John Home to send for a post-chaise and carry them out to Musselburgh, which was done directly, and which relieved us from all troublesome company.'

It is a very unpleasant story, and one hardly knows which is

relate to their own edification and comfort; and I have no doubt of its being found, upon inquiry, that the ministerial duties of preaching, examination, visiting the sick, etc., are generally performed with more exemplary diligence and regularity in parishes where the dissenting interest has got footing, and the parishioners enjoy the opportunity of choosing between the Church and the Secession.

'But supposing these advantages to be conceded, are they not counterbalanced by the animosity, the spleen, the censorious and malevolent spirit, nourished by schismatical principles? In reply to this insinuation, I am now to state what at first view may appear paradoxical, but what I really believe to be a fact, namely, that diversity of religious opinions and sects have promoted charity, and the more active and habitual exercise of the virtues of candour, meekness, and forbearance. These virtues, dormant and sluggish in a monotonous state of external religious unanimity, are called forth, and always more eminently displayed in instances where legal toleration has given unrestrained scope to freedom of sentiment, and diversity of religious names and institutions.' *My Life and Times*, pp. 86-8.

H

worse: Carlyle's action at the time, or the way in which more
than thirty years afterwards he recalls it, and sets it down
without a blush or a twinge of regret.

To turn to something much pleasanter. The *Old Statistical
Account* written by the various parish ministers in Scotland
under the direction of Sir John Sinclair of Ulbster (whose
swaggering portrait by Raeburn is one of the glories of our
National Gallery), is extremely valuable not only as a description of the country in the last decade of the eighteenth century, but often as a most interesting, and at times amusing,
revelation of the character of the various contributors.

The following two short extracts from the account by Carlyle, of the parish of Inveresk, may give us some taste of this
quality.

'The fishwives' manner of life and the business of making
their markets, whet their faculties and make them very dex-
terous in bargain-making. They have likewise a species of rude
eloquence, an extreme facility in expressing their feelings by
words or gestures, which is very imposing, and enables them to
carry their points even against the most wary, and they are too
well acquainted with the world to be abashed when they are
detected in any of their arts. . .

'The inhabitants [of the parish] are in general contented and
unambitious, and would always be so, did not their constant
intercourse with the capital, which is of so much advantage to
them in other respects, expose them to the false arts of inde-
fatigable seducers, who, under pretence of Reform, wish to
subvert the present happy government, and introduce demo-
cratical anarchy in its stead.'

Carlyle was too big, in body and mind, to be a snob or a syco-
phant, but he was truly an eighteenth-century man in his
reverence for people of high social rank. He loved their company, and delighted in the impression that he was able to make
upon them. Here is a fragment from his account of a visit
to Archibald, third Duke of Argyll, at that time Lord Justice
General of Scotland, the judge at the famous 'Appin Murder'
trial in 1752 who by a strongly biased charge to a packed jury

of his own clan[1] sent James Stewart of the Glens—in all probability quite innocent of the crime—to his death.

'The provisions for the table [at Inveraray Castle] were at least equal to the conversation; for we had sea and river fish in perfection, the best beef and mutton and fowls and wild game and venison of both kinds in abundance. The wines, too, were excellent.

'I stayed over Sunday, and preached to his Grace, who always attended the church at Inveraray. The ladies told me that I had pleased his Grace, which gratified me not a little, as without him no preferment could be obtained in Scotland . . . I may add here, that when he died in spring 1761, it was found that he had marked my name down in his private note-book for Principal of the College of Glasgow, a body in whose prosperity he was much interested, as he had been educated there, and had said to Andrew Fletcher junior, to whom he showed the note, that it would be very hard if he and I between us could not manage that troublesome society. This took no effect, for the Duke died a year or two before Principal Campbell, when Lord Bute had all the power.'

One wonders if this sermon at Inveraray was at all like that which, as he tells, he had preached one Sunday at Athelstaneford for his friend John Home, when David Hume was in church. 'When we met before dinner, "What did you mean," says he to me, "by treating John's congregation to-day with one of Cicero's academics?" I did not think that such heathen morality would have passed in East Lothian.' Another remark may be recalled of that same shrewd critic about a simple and earnest discourse he once chanced to hear John Brown of Haddington preach:

'That man spoke as if he was conscious that the Son of God stood at his elbow.'[2]

It would, however, be an utter injustice to Carlyle to reckon him as simply like the hireling shepherds Milton scarifies in *Lycidas*:

[1] 'Before a Campbell jury and a Campbell judge, and that in a Campbell country and upon a Campbell quarrel!' R. L. Stevenson, *Catriona*, p. 20.

[2] Life of Dr Waugh, p. 52.

Of other care they little reckoning make
Than how to scramble at the shearers' feast,
And shove away the worthy bidden guest.
Blind mouths! that scarce themselves know how to hold
A sheep-hook, or have learn'd aught else the least
That to the faithful herdman's art belongs!

No one can read the *Autobiography*, frank as it is almost to cynicism in its judgements of men and in the writer's revelation of himself, without feeling oneself in contact with a very strong and virile personality, with real kindliness and loyalty to his friends, a mind keenly awake and interested in his fellow-men, with a thorough knowledge of them on every side but the spiritual, and an uncanny talent for managing them.

I think in all probability he had got in early youth a twist against Evangelical Religion so far as its outward expression was concerned. It has been suggested that this may have been due to what he saw in a near neighbour, James Erskine, of Grange, whose life was of the strangest *Jekyll and Hyde* order; an Ultra-Presbyterian, yet up to the neck in Jacobite plots; a Lord of Session yet arranging with an even greater villain than himself, Simon Fraser, Lord Lovat, for the kidnapping of his own wife, who was probably insane, and carrying her off to St Kilda; a man who while his private life was steeped in debauchery, kept a diary full of the most pietistic expressions. 'It is the diary', says John Hill Burton[1] 'of a haunted mind, keeping up its religious fervour to drive out other thoughts, and seems to march on in its adopted tone,

> Like one that on a lonesome road
> Doth walk in fear and dread,
> And having once turn'd round, walks on,
> And turns no more his head;
> Because he knows, a frightful fiend
> Doth close behind him tread.

Such was Lord Grange.'

Whether this conjecture be true or not, the fact remains that in the *Autobiography* Carlyle hardly ever refers to the Evangeli-

[1] *History of Scotland*, viii, p. 396.

cal party without a sneer or a snarl. But there are unexpected qualities in him of which the *Autobiography* reveals little or nothing. Who would have imagined that the formidable 'Jupiter', the unwearied antagonist to all 'High-flyers' and every kind of manifestation of 'Enthusiasm', should, at a time when to open a Sabbath School was, at best, considered an 'unnecessary and dangerous' act, and, at worst, rendered oneself liable to be summoned before the Sheriff, and when in certain parishes parents who had sent their children to such a school were threatened with deprivation of Church Ordinances,[1] who would have imagined, I say, that Carlyle was a pioneer in such work in Scotland? Yet this stands in the record:

'Inveresk, 1st August 1790.

'At this sederunt, the Following Proposal was laid before the Session by the Moderator—That whereas it has been Found from experience That Many of the Children of the Lower Rank in this Parish, Tho' they have learn'd to Read in their Infancy, yet Thro' negligence or their Being early engag'd in some Business, are in Danger of Entirely forgetting what they have been Taught;

'And whereas the New School for Teaching Young Girls a branch of Manufacture, However useful in other Respects, necessarily occupies all their time in week Days, and makes it Impossible for them to attend Masters for Reading and the Principles of Religion;

'And whereas Multitudes of Children of both sexes are allow'd to Run about Idle the Whole Lord's Day, which tends to Breed them not only in Ignorance, but to Irreverence for Religious Institutions, and consequently to Dissolute Manners, it is Thought that a Sunday's School or two in this Parish which have been found of so much use in Populous Towns, will help to correct Those abuses, and to prevent these Evils;

'It is therefore proposed, That an attempt shall be made immediately to form such an institution.

---

[1] The Duke of Atholl of that day insisted that an Act of Parliament was the only method against 'meetings under the name of Sunday Schools, where the lowest of the people become teachers, and are instilling into the minds of the rising generation the most pernicious doctrines both civil and religious'. Quoted in *Christian Freedom*, Dr W. M. Macgregor, p. 233*n*.

'The same Day, the Session, Having taken the above proposal into their Serious consideration, unanimously agreed thereto, and Resolved to send Subscription Papers to such Persons as may be able and willing to promote such a Pious undertaking, That an annual sum may be rais'd to pay Sallaries to two Masters, one in Musselburgh and another in Fisherrow, and to Defray all other charges that may be necessary.   ALEX. CARLYLE.'

He at once set to work levying Subscriptions in the parish—Lady Hailes, Five Guineas, the Duchess of Buccleuch, Ten Pounds, Lady Hope, Three Guineas, etc.—and drew up very sensible rules for the schools, and those in charge of them, e.g. '(3rdly) That they [the two teachers] shall receive no more than 50 a Piece at a time, as it would be Impossible to teach a greater number at once. . . (8thly) That every young person shall attend the School in their best Cloaths, That they are all to behave in an Orderly and submissive manner, and that such as do not, shall be expunged from the List and admitted no more.'

Two instances, also somewhat unexpected, of Dr Carlyle's friendly relations with his Seceder neighbour, Rev. Alex. Black, shed a gracious light upon the finer qualities of his spirit.

Dr Carlyle to Rev. Alex. Black, Minister of the Associate Secession Chapel, Newbigging, Musselburgh.

'Mussh., Dec. 25, 1798.

'Revd and Dear Sir,—

'I return you many thanks for the excellent sermon which you sent me, and which I perus'd once and again with entire satisfaction: not merely on account of the manner in which it is executed, but for the warm Patriot Spirit which it Breathes, and the very necessary and animated caution which it gives against Lay Preachers, which I hold to be one of the most Dangerous symptoms of the Times. I was extremely well pleas'd with the Appendix also, and am in Doubt whether I should most admire the splendid Paragraphs it contains, or the Friendly Candour in annexing it to your own Work. I am truly proud that so Pious and Patriotick a Sermon is the Production of my Parish, of the sincerity of which Profession you

will not Doubt when I tell you that I sent it yesterday under
cover to the Right Honble Mr Secretary Dundas, as a speci-
men of the Present Sentiments of the Ministers of our Denomi-
nation.—I am, with Sincere Regard, Revd and Dear Sir,
Yours, Etc.   ALEXR CARLYLE.

P.S. I have only two of my Printed Sermons bye me at
present, which I beg you to accept of.'

'Manse Mush., July 10. 1803.

'Revd and Dear Sir, I have the satisfaction herewith of
transmitting to you and your Session from the Session of the
Parish of Inveresk, a Laver or Baptismal Bason, for the use of
your Chapel, of which we beg your acceptance.

'The Frank Goodwill with which you offer'd us your Chapel
for assembling those of the Establish'd Church for Publick
Worship, for a part of every Lord's Day, while the Parish
Church is Rebuilding, Demanded some lasting mark of ac-
knowledgement from us, And it is our Special Wish and Prayer
to Almighty God that you may Long Continue to exercise your
Holy Function with the same Respect and Success which you
have hitherto enjoy'd.

'The Publick Danger, now so Imminent, Diminishes in a
great Degree, to nothing almost, any small Differences in
opinion that may be between us, and magnifies those Many
Essential Points in which we agree, and Tends to Lessen our
Distance from each other.

'In one Important Christian Grace, That of Benevolence and
Brotherly Love, we are of one accord. In this you have lately
made the advance, and set us an Example, which has excit'd
in us a Mutual Regard which I trust will never cease.

'This I write in my own name and in that of the Session of
Inveresk with every kind wish for Temporal and Spiritual
Blessings to you and all your Flock.—I am, with sincere esteem,
Revd and Dear Sir, Your affectionate Brother and most hum-
ble Servt, ALEXR CARLYLE.'

Then one short letter to Mrs Black, written a little over a
year before his death, when he was an old man of eighty-two,
shows the pleasant comings and goings between the Manses.

'Dr Carlyle presents his compliments to Mrs Black, and begs
her acceptance of a few Bottles Sweet Wine for her children,

wh. a Thousand Thanks for the use of her House with so much
freedom to him and his Friends, and not without Inconveni-
ency to her and her Family. The Dr sends his kindest Compliments to Mr Black.'

Extracts like these with all their quaint formality show
plainly that ecclesiastical Scotland in the days of our great
grandfathers—as well as in many pleasant memories of those
of us who are younger—was not always the Bear-Garden or
Cock-pit it has sometimes been represented to have been by
historians whose imaginations or whose prejudices make them
blind to the facts.

One last quotation will show how the fire that was in him
broke out in an Assembly speech the year before his death. An
address to the King had been prepared, in the Babylonish jar-
gon customary in such documents—and this expression occurred in it—'*the awful situation of the Country*'. Scarcely had the
Clerk ceased reading when the old man leapt to his feet.

'Moderator, [he said] I was so unlucky as not to be able to
attend the Committee who drew up this Address, and consequently have heard it now for the first time. In general I am
well pleased with the Address. But there is one phrase in it,
which has just now been read, that I do not like. I do not like
to have it known to our enemies by a public act of this Assembly, that we think our country in an awful state, which implies
more terror and dismay than I am willing to own. When the
Almighty wields the Elements, which are His instruments of
vengeance on guilty nations—when heaven's thunders roll and
envelop the world in fire—when the furious tempest rages, and
whelms triumphant navies in the deep—when the burning
mountain disgorges its fiery entrails and lays populous cities in
ashes;—then, indeed, I am overawed: I acknowledge the right
arm of the Almighty: I am awed into reverence and fear: I am
still and feel that he is God: I am dumb, and open not my
mouth. But when a puny mortal, of no better materials than
myself, struts and frets and fumes and menaces, then am I
roused but not overawed; I put myself in array against the
vain boaster, and am ready to say with the high priest of the
poet, *I fear God and have no other fear*.'

This is the authentic Olympian thunder—yes, and something better, something that we would all welcome and be the better for hearing to-day, alike in Church and State.

And here we may take leave of the stout-hearted old Minister of Inveresk. He retained his bodily and mental vigour to the end. No reader of the *Autobiography* would ever imagine that the author was a man of seventy-nine when he set pen to paper and that he had nothing but his vivid and tenacious memory to help him. Page after page of his beautifully firm and legible writing may be read in the Session Records of the congregation.

As a young man he had dabbled in poetry—not very successfully, though in some verses there are distinct echoes of Collins's lovely *Ode to Evening*—that ode with its magical verse:

Now air is hush'd save where the weak-eyed bat
With short shrill shriek flits by on leathern wing,
    Or where the beetle winds
    His small but sullen horn.

Needless to say, Carlye has nothing to equal this. But in *An Ode To the Memory of Colonel Gardiner, In Imitation of Milton*, which it is practically certain was written by him, there are lines which present a curious literary problem, for, word for word, they are identical with the famous *Ode Written in 1746* by Collins:

How sleep the brave, who sink to rest,
By all their country's wishes blest!

Which of the two men must be adjudged the borrower? In extreme old age he wrote an extraordinarily interesting appreciation of Wordsworth's *The Brothers* and *The Idiot Boy*: 'On reading *The Brothers* I was surprised at first with its simplicity or rather flatness. But when I got a little on, I found it not only raised my curiosity but moved me into sympathy. . . After being so affected, could I deny that this was poetry, however simply expressed?' Again on *The Idiot Boy*—'I offered my thanks to the God of Poets for having inspired one of his sons with a new species of poetry, and for having pointed out a subject on which the author has done more to move the human heart to tenderness for the most unfortunate of our species than has ever been done before.'

We remember Jeffrey's famous and unlucky pronouncement on *The Excursion* in *The Edinburgh Review*, beginning 'This will never do!' and are thankful to discover that in a most unexpected quarter a true appreciation of a new and strange type of poetry was manifesting itself.

How far Carlyle was a typical Moderate, may be a matter of debate. No doubt, there were many ministers of the party who 'did justly, and loved mercy, and walked humbly with God'— men of the fine type of Dr Somerville of Jedburgh, whose *My Life and Times*, covering practically the same period as Carlyle, should always be read along with the Autobiography; or the kindly Scholar, George Ridpath, of Stitchel, 'judicious and learned' as Carlyle calls him, who lived for the writing of his *History of the Borders*; or, best known of all, the Rev. Micah Balwhidder in Galt's *Annals of the Parish*—a much more life-like and lovable figure, in my judgement, than the *Vicar of Wakefield* himself.

But there were others, who, it is no want of charity to say, were in their 'office for a piece of bread',—'moderate in ability, showing a moderate degree of zeal, and doing a very moderate amount of work', as I once heard it put—content to follow the line of least resistance, and bringing no credit to their church, even if they did not sink so low as did some of their gross, greedy, and tyrannical contemporaries in the Church of England who were pilloried for ever by Hogarth and Rowlandson and Gilray. For such as they, least said, soonest mended. Let the dead—dead in every sense of the term—bury their dead:

There was—there is—something in Moderatism at its best that appeals to a very typical element in Scottish character: its caution, its reticence on religious matters, its impatience with what is merely emotional, a certain dogged tenacity and love of ordered discipline, which from the dawn of history has struggled within every Scot and will continue to struggle to the end, with that other element: idealist and adventurous, which for a good cause will 'throw its cap over the mill', and never dream of looking over its shoulder to see whether many are following, or few. Jupiter Carlyle and the party of which he was so distinguished and whole-hearted a member, had little or nothing of this latter element, but they undoubtedly have their place in the history and development of the Scottish nation.

Of his outward appearance we have abundant record. Here is a description of him on one of his missions on Church affairs to London. 'His portly figure, his fine expressive countenance with an aquiline nose, his flowing silver locks and the freshness of the colour of his face, made a prodigious impression on the courtiers.' We can see him in the prime of his manly beauty in the portrait by David Martin, pupil of Allan Ramsay and master of Raeburn[1]; in two portraits by Archibald Skirving in the National Portrait Gallery, one a noble profile, like one of the greatest of the Roman Emperors, the other in his formidable old age—the debater who took the General Assembly by the throat; and, perhaps the most characteristic of all, the etching by John Kay. 'This limner', says Burton, 'had the peculiar faculty, while preserving a recognizable likeness, of entirely divesting it of every vestige of grace or picturesqueness, which nature may have bestowed upon it.' But be that as it may, I always feel in turning over *Kay's Portraits* that, bad as the drawing often is, *thus and thus the men*—Kames and Monboddo, Dr Erskine dangling his glove, or the gigantic Highland Chief, Francis McNab, reeling down the North Bridge, and all the rest of them—*were seen by their contemporaries.* And here we have Carlyle: a tall, upright, squire-like figure in top-boots and spurs, riding-whip in hand, and wearing a wide-skirted horseman's coat over his professional black garments, with nothing else to mark the minister but the broad bands, which it was the fashion of the time to wear, out of the pulpit, as well as in it.[2]

The exact image of the man himself is, of course, that which

---

[1] Prefixed to the *Autobiography*.

[2] He also sat in the summer of 1796 to Raeburn for a portrait commissioned by the Earl of Haddington. So far as I know, this has not been engraved or photographed, nor is there any mention of it in the catalogues of Raeburn's pictures. If it still exists, it is probably at Tyninghame or Mellerstain.

is revealed in page after page of the *Autobiography*. He is not in the least a hero to himself, but still less has he any so-called 'inferiority complex'. He can never be classed among the great men of the Scottish Church. He left no successor in the General Assembly, and when he died, a great change was already beginning to manifest itself throughout Church and State alike. There was no rainbow in his sky, and his spiritual influence was negligible. But what a vigorous old fellow he is, and, when all is said and done, how likeable!—alive in every fibre of him, and, no matter what company he is in, dominating it with easy and unconscious power.

I frankly confess that, with every one of my political and ecclesiastical traditions and prejudices, inherited and acquired, against Jupiter Carlyle and all that he stood for, I close one more of many readings of the famous *Autobiography* with a very definite liking for the man, and an ever-deepening admiration for the writer, who has made eighteenth-century Scotland pass so vividly before my eyes.

A REFORMATION DIARIST
AND HIS TIMES

AS we look back over the history of Scotland during the latter half of the eventful sixteenth century—the century that marked the birth of Modern Europe—one great commanding figure rises up, dwarfing almost every other, stirring up among many the fiercest hatred, but winning from far more an equally passionate devotion—the figure of John Knox. But the work of Knox, epoch-making as it was, was not done single-handed. In many respects he was but a pioneer. When the unfinished task fell from his hands in 1572, it was taken up and shaped and brought to marvellous completeness by other men, less known to us nowadays, perhaps, but none the less deserving of remembrance.

The man on whom the mantle and a double portion of the spirit of John Knox fell, was Andrew Melvill. Great in himself, he was great also in contrast with many of those with whom he had to do. One of the most distinguished scholars in Europe, yet a man of ready practical resource; perpetually engaged in controversy, yet capable of inspiring the most ardent personal affection; at one time by far the most powerful man in Scotland, yet, after a life of seven-and-seventy stormy adventurous years, dying in obscurity and exile: such in barest outline was his life. Fortunately the task of filling in the outline is by no means difficult, because for the greater part of the story we have the *Diary* of his nephew and close companion, James Melvill, to guide us. This book is not nearly so well known as it ought to be. True, there are many arid tracts in it, and the outward form is repellent to a degree. But, as when a certain foolish man once brought a brother to see Dr Johnson, saying, 'When we have sat together some time, you'll find my brother grow very entertaining,' Johnson answered, 'Sir, I can wait'; so, after a little waiting and judicious skipping of the *Diary* we have our reward, for much of the book is wholly delightful, the author's goodness, gentleness, and humour shining out on many a page. It is written in a charming desultory fashion in the raciest of Angus Scotch, the dialect still in familiar use in the Montrose near which Melvill was born and spent his youth. To know him aright, indeed, you must know that town of the 'Gable endies', with its streets swept by the keen east wind. The natural features are still the same; the narrow peninsula running north and south between the North and the South Esk, with the glorious links and broad sea beach to the east, and to the west that singular lagoon, the Montrose Basin, for one half the day an abhorrent stretch of black mud, with a few mussel-gatherers busy at their work; for the other half, filled with the incoming tide, 'brimming and bright and large', like Oxus, while the big rounded hills of Wirren and the Bulg keep watch beyond.

Sloping down to the southern margin of the *Aestuarium fluminis Aeskae meridionalis*—such being the weight of bad Latin which the Montrose Basin had to bear in the sixteenth century —are the fields of the little estate of Baldovy, in the mansion-house of which, now vanished, Andrew Melvill was born on 1 August 1545. He was the youngest of nine brothers, and early lost his father who fell in 1547 at Pinkie, fighting gallantly against the English in 'a battle which made many orphans'. The estate was very small, and in those impoverished times it could not support a large family, many of whose members were already grown up. On the father's death it passed to the eldest son, Richard, minister of Maryton, the parish in which Baldovy is situated, and in his manse Andrew Melvill was brought up. There was a difference in age of some three-and-twenty years between the two brothers, and Andrew was thus more like a son than a brother in the household. His mother did not long survive her husband, but her place was taken by Richard Melvill's wife, who treated Andrew 'maist lovingly and tenderly'. He was 'a sickly tender boy and took pleasure in naething sae mickle as his buik', his nephew tells us. But as he grew up, he slowly gained strength in the long quiet days in Maryton woods. His brother had known George Wishart intimately and had studied under Melanchthon at Wittenberg. So when the Reformation came, he threw himself heart and soul into the good cause. Doubtless he was influenced also by the fact that one of the leaders in that cause was another intimate friend, John Erskine of Dun, whose house lies on the sunny face of the hill across the Basin, right opposite to Baldovy. The two houses became the haunt of the more famous Reformers, and thus Andrew Melvill was brought much into contact with them at the most impressionable age.

Montrose was the first place in Scotland where Greek was taught, and so thoroughly did Melvill profit by the teaching of Petrus de Marsiliers in its Grammar School, that when at the age of fourteen he entered St Andrews University, he was able to read Aristotle in the original, much to the astonishment of professors and students alike, who knew only the Latin version.

He passed through his course there, and left with a brilliant reputation as 'the best philosopher, poet and Grecian of any young maister in the land'. Then, with the keen thirst for knowledge so characteristic of his age, he resolved to go to France and study in Paris. Thither accordingly he went, being 'by the way', as his nephew tells us, 'extremely tormented with sea-sickness and storm of weather, so that oft-times he looked for death', as many others have done in like circumstances since. Reaching Dieppe safely, however, he *walked* to Paris—100 miles—and there for the present we shall leave him.

His nephew James, with whom he was to be closely associated in after days, was at this time about eight years old. He was the youngest of Richard Melvill's sons. His mother had died when he was a mere infant, but there was something in the boy, as in the man in after years, that won people's hearts. As he very simply says: 'I cam never to the place but God moved some ane with a motherly affection towards me.' He was sent to school at Logie Manse, which is still standing: the old rooms may still be seen where the boys learned their lessons. The master was William Gray, the minister of Logie; his sister kept house, and as Melvill says, 'was a very loving mother to us indeed'. The minister read Latin and spoke French with the boys, and in active pursuits gave them an excellent all-round training, for, James says, 'by our maister we were teached to handle the bow for archery, the glub for goff, the batons for fencing, also to rin, to loup, to swoom, to warstle, to preve pratteiks[1]—every ane having his match and antagonist, baith in our lessons and play. A happy and golden time indeed, until the pest came to Montrose: so that the school skailled, and we were all sent for and brought hame.' A charming picture this is, of education in the quiet of the remote country in the old days when news travelled slowly of all the wild doings in Edinburgh—the marriage of Mary and Darnley, the slaughter of 'Signor Davie' (Rizzio), the birth of James VI—when the boys were taken out to see the beacon lighted on Montrose Steeple—the 'King's' murder, and the Queen's defeat and flight into England.

James remained for a time at home, and then, like his uncle, went to Montrose Grammar School. There he made very considerable progress in his studies, and at the same time showed a healthy love of mischief, as he tells us in his Diary with a certain regretful complacency, not uncommon in douce men of mature years. His father, a man of strong and austere character, held in much awe by the whole household, wished him to stay at home and help in the work of the farm, and for a while James did so. But his whole heart was in the scholar's life, in desire to enter the ministry, and to go to St Andrews University as a preparation for it. He tells us how one day, coming from Maryton Smithy with some reaping-hooks for the harvest, he fell on his knees and prayed that his father might be moved to send him to college. The prayer was answered, for within a few days one of the 'regents' of St Leonard's College, St Andrews, came to Baldovy, and finding out the boy's secret, persuaded his father to let him enter as a student under his care. 'Rebecca', says Melvill, 'was never blyther to go with the servant of Abraham nor I was to go with him.' He was only fifteen years of age, and, like many another country lad, though fairly well grounded, he found the town-bred boys ahead of him, and his master's lessons on Logic and Rhetoric too abstract and crabbed for him to grasp.

---

[1] I do not quite know what this means. Jamieson gives *To prieve pratteiks* = *to attempt tricks*. If this is so, one can only admire the breadth of the curriculum at Logie in its inclusion of a subject in which, one might think, most boys require no special instruction.

'I was cast in sic a grief and despair because I understood not his language, that I did naething but bursted and grat at his lessons, and was of mind to have gone hame again, but the loving care of that man comforted me, and took me in his ain chalmer . . . and every night teached me in private till I was acquainted with the matter. Mairower in these years I learned my music, wherein I took greater delight of ane Alexander Smith servant to the Primarius of our college wha had been trained up amang the monks in the Abbey. I learned of him the gam, plain-song and monie of the trebles of the Psalms, whereof some I could weill sing in the Kirk; but my naturalitie and easy learning by the ear made me the mair unsolid and unready to use the form of the art. I lovit singing and playing on instruments passing weill, and would gladly spend time whar the exercise thereof was within the College: for twa or three of our condisciples played fellon weill on the virginals and another on the lute and gittern. Our Regent had also the pinalds [spinet] in his chamber and learnit some thing and I after him; but perceiving me ower mickle carried after that, he dishanted and left off. It was the great mercy of my God that keipit me from any great progress in singing and playing on instruments; for, gif I had attained to any reasonable measure therein, I had never done gude otherways.'

But there was something better at St Andrews than Logic or Music lessons. Who does not know the fascination of that old town; its streets radiating from the Cathedral; the castle on the cliff with its Bottle Dungeon, the old colleges of St Salvator and St Leonard and St Mary; and the grey sea outside, where the French had come and carried off Knox and his friends? Years had passed since that event, and as the students of Melvill's day—mere boys as they were—wandered in their scarlet gowns along the streets after class hours, they would see a thin, stooping figure dressed in fur-lined cloak and with long iron-grey beard sweeping down to his girdle, who would sometimes call the boys to him as he rested in St Leonard's Yard, and bless them, exhorting them to know God and His work in the country, and stand by the good cause. This was John Knox, driven from Edinburgh for the time being by the jealousy of Regent Morton. Feeble though the old man seemed, as he

I

sunned himself in the College Yard, every Sabbath in the Parish Kirk he showed that his spirit was as strong as ever. Melvill tells us how he heard him lecture on the Book of Daniel:

'In the opening up of his text he was moderate the space of an half hour, but when he entered to application he made me sae to grew and tremble that I could not haud a pen to write . . . I saw him every day of his doctrine go hulie and fear, with a furring of martriks about his neck, a staff in the ane hand, and guid godly Richard Ballanden, his servant, hauding up the other oxter, from the Abbey to the Parish Kirk; and by the said Richard and another servant lifted up to the pulpit whar he behovit to lean at his first entry: but or he had done with his sermon he was so active and vigorous that he was like to ding that pulpit in blads and fly out of it!'

Meanwhile Andrew Melvill had been lost sight of by his friends. Ten years had passed since he last saw Scotland. It was known that he had left Paris, and had gone to Poictiers. But France was distracted by war, and it was feared that—outspoken Protestant as he was known to be—he had perished in the tumults following the Massacre of St Bartholomew. After hope had been given up, however, a Scottish refugee arrived from Geneva, bearing letters from him to his brother at Baldovy, and the letters were soon followed by the writer himself, to the great joy especially of his nephew James. Henceforward the two men were to be connected in the closest and most intimate relations. All through, James showed the most beautiful admiration of his uncle and loyalty to him, speaking of himself as 'ane wha wald to God he war as like to Mr Andro in gifts of mind, as he is thought to be in proportion of body and lineaments of face: for there is nane that is nocht otherways particularly informed but taks me for Mr Andro's brother.' It will be seen how admirably each helped the other, how with common sympathies and a common aim, each had different methods of work: James the *suaviter in modo*, Andrew the *fortiter in re*; while both were actuated by the noblest Christian patriotism and a passionate love of liberty, as against all tyranny whether of king, or noble, or bishop. Of James there exists no

portrait, except that drawn unconsciously by himself in the
pages of his Diary. A most charming portrayal it is, of a singularly sweet and happy nature. In the University of Sedan there
is still shown a portrait of Andrew: an acute Calvin-like face,
with strongly marked aquiline features, and short pointed beard.
Like Knox, he was a little man, spare in person, and active in
habit, capable of walking feats that would now shame the
most athletic.

His life in France and Geneva was very typical of 'the Scot
Abroad' in those days. The first two years in Paris were spent
in incessant study whereby he added to his already great
stores of learning, especially in Hebrew and Greek; in the
latter tongue he lectured regularly, 'uttering never a word but
Greek with sic readiness and plenty as was marvellous to the
hearers.' He then went to Poictiers to study Law and Theology.
While he was there, war broke out. The great Admiral Coligny
besieged the town, and the classes were broken up. But Melvill
stayed on as tutor in the family of one of the magistrates. He
always got on well with boys and young men, and a great
affection sprang up between him and the magistrate's only son.
When the poor boy was killed in the siege by a shot from a
cannon, he died in Melvill's arms, crying out in Greek,
'Master, I have finished my course.' 'That bairn', says James,
'gaed never out of his heart, but in teaching of me he often
remembered him with tender compassion of mind.'

After the siege was raised, Andrew started to walk across
France to Geneva—some three hundred miles. His luggage
was probably as limited as tourist ever took: consisting solely
of a little Hebrew Bible at his belt. He kept his eyes open as he
went. 'His companions of the way,' we are told, 'when they
cam to the inn, wald lie down like tired tykes, but he wald out
and sight the towns and villages whithersoever they cam.'[1]

[1] One remembers that earlier picture of the travelling Scot in the Twelfth
Century—Abbot (then brother) Samson going to Rome and undergoing
many perils by the way. 'I, however, pretended to be Scotch, and putting
on the garb of a Scotchman, and taking the gesture of one, walked along;
and when anybody mocked at me, I would brandish my staff in the manner
of that weapon they call *gaveloc*, uttering comminatory words after the way
of the Scotch.' Carlyle, *Past and Present*, p. 61.

When they reached Geneva, his one remaining companion, a Frenchman, remembering that there was 'but a crown to the fore betwixt them baith,' sought to soften the porter's heart by saying 'We are poor scholars'. But Geneva was already over-run with those who so described themselves, and 'Mr Andro', who, as truly as Burns, believed in 'garring our streams and burnies shine up wi' the best', said boldly, 'No, no, we are not poor! We have as mickle as will pay for all we tak, as lang as we tarry.' But he had what was better than money: good Scots wit, and letters to Beza, Calvin's successor. Beza set him to teach in the University for two or three days on trial, and Melvill acquitted himself so well in this test that Geneva was glad to retain his services for five years. Busy years they were, with new studies and new ideas. Geneva was at that time a hot-bed of Radicalism to which Melvill took with right good will. He made new friends also, among others a Greek professor—Greek by birth—with whom he had many arguments as to the correct pronunciation of the Greek's own language. Melvill, like a true Scot, was absolutely sure that his own way was right, and characteristically gave all sorts of reasons for this assurance, till the Greek lost his temper, and perhaps also his command of the Latin in which the strange disputation was carried on, and shouted—'You Scotchmen, you barbarians, have you the impudence to teach us Greeks the pronunciation of our own tongue?'

At length letters from Scotland, especially one from his nephew, changed all his plans, and though Geneva was exceedingly loath to lose one who, at the age of twenty-eight, was already in the very front rank of the scholars and theologians of Europe,[1] in a happy hour for Scotland he determined to return, and after many adventures and narrow escapes as he crossed France, reached his native land in safety in the summer of 1574.

His fame had preceded him, and various doors were ready to open for him; but knowing his own powers and seeing the

[1] Theodore Beza wrote: 'The greatest token of affection the Kirk of Geneva could show to Scotland is that they have suffered themselves to be spoiled of Mr Andrew Melvill.'

low state in which education then was in Scotland, he determined to put out all his strength for his Kirk and country. So
he declined a good position at court, and after spending a few
months at Baldovy, where he and his nephew were inseparable
companions in study and recreation, he accepted the Principalship of Glasgow University.

It was no light task to which he bent himself. The classes
had not been held for several years; the finances of the University were in a state of chaos, and there was no one as yet to
whom Melvill could look for assistance in teaching. But he had
invincible courage and a constitution of steel, and having got
together a few young men as students, without more ado he
put them through a six years' course, teaching them Greek,
Latin, Mathematics, Astronomy, Geography, Moral Philosophy, Physics, History, Hebrew, Chaldee, Theology (Calvin's
Institutes), and in addition, lectured on the whole Bible.

How mortal man could know all these subjects, and even in
six years teach them, is almost impossible to imagine, but
Melvill was a man of relentless thoroughness, both with himself and with those whom he taught. Soon his fame began to
spread, and the once deserted class-rooms were crowded with
students who came from all parts of the country to sit under
this dauntless little professor, who had proved himself able
single-handed to carry on a whole University curriculum. Before long, however, he was able to delegate the more elemen-
tary parts of the course to several of his pupils, and his nephew
James took complete charge of the department of Mathematics.
But the Principal's hand was everywhere felt, and nowhere
more than in the sternness of his discipline. James Melvill has
many a racy story of how 'my uncle, Mr Andro' dealt with
some of his young ruffians of students. But we must pass on to
what was perhaps the greatest work of his life, continued for
many years, often at great personal risk for which he cared not
a jot: namely, his struggle with the King and his advisers
against interference with the freedom of the Church and the
introduction of Episcopacy.

The Presbyterian form of government in the Scottish Church
owes much to Melvill. Of course, in its main outline Presby-

terianism is of older origin; but in its final drafting, in its careful 'redding of the marches' between Church and State, Melvill's hand is clearly seen. The legal precision which his studies at Paris and Poictiers had given him, and the love of liberty which, as in every true Scot, was ingrained in the very marrow of his bones, and which his five years in Geneva had only intensified, are both seen in the great *Second Book of Discipline*, as it is called, over which much of the battle was fought, with varying fortune, for more than five-and-twenty years.

Let it be briefly indicated how the state of affairs came to be as it was. In the pre-Reformation Church there had been bishops, many of whom had seats in Parliament. After the Reformation and the establishment of Presbytery, the old bishoprics were filled, as vacancies occurred, by Protestant ministers, and sometimes by laymen. But much of the Episcopal revenues had been confiscated, and what remained, though legally due to the bishops alone, was demanded by the nobles for themselves. Accordingly, bishops were appointed who had the title and drew the revenue, which, however, they did not *keep*, but handed over to their patrons, receiving from them a greater or less stipend in return. The bishops were thus mere men of straw, and a bitter gibe of the time dubbed them *Tulchans*. That was the name given then in Scotland to the erection of wood stuffed with straw and covered with calf-skin, which the sagacious dairy farmer of that time thrust beside a cow to make her give her milk more freely. This sham episcopacy had been set up some two years before Andrew Melvill's return to Scotland, and from the first he set his face like a flint against it. Because of this opposition and for other independent acts, he became very obnoxious to James Douglas, Earl of Morton, 'James the Reeve' as he was called, who was the last of the four Regents who held the reins of government during the minority of James VI. Morton was 'one of the grimmest figures even of the grim race from which he sprang— profligate, merciless, unscrupulous, yet he was not a mere lawless desperado'.[1] In short he was, in many ways, the very antithesis of Andrew Melvill, and the two strong-willed men soon

[1] Hume Brown, *History of Scotland*, ii, 181.

came into sharp collision. A portrait of Morton in the possession of his descendants at Dalmahoy House shows a strong, thick-set figure in black doublet and trunk-hose, with high-crowned black steeple hat carelessly stuck on the back of his head; the face ruddy, with high cheek bones and short red beard—a true Red Douglas; one hand is on his hip, the other resting on the pommel of his sword; the whole aspect and attitude of the man showing ruthless determination.

He could be very courteous and suave when he pleased, and at first he tried to win Melvill by fair words and bribes. But when he found these of no avail, he lost his temper and broke out: 'There will never be quietness in this country till half a dizzen of you be hangit, or banished the country.' 'Tush, sir,' says Mr Andro, 'threaten your purple minions in that way. It is all one to me whether I rot in the air or underground. The earth is the Lord's, and it will not lie in your power to hang or exile His truth.'

Meanwhile, King James was growing up to man's estate, and it will be well for us to get some idea of what manner of man he was. Of the better, sunnier side of his character we have the brilliant sketch in *The Fortunes of Nigel*. But there was another side, as both Scotland and England found to their cost.

It was an age when the very strictest economy of truth was professed and practised in affairs of State, but even the greatest masters in *Kingcraft*, as it was euphemistically called, acknowledged that James's powers of sheer unmitigated lying were far beyond those of any of his contemporaries. He delighted in crooked ways and little meannesses. He was utterly without personal dignity, and coarse and drunken in his habits. Yet he possessed much natural shrewdness, very considerable scholarship, a great fondness for, and skill in, theological discussion, and a power of reading the signs of the times and of summing up a situation in a pithy and memorable phrase, which his grave and decorous son Charles utterly lacked. Yet all his life long he was under the influence of worthless favourites. His character is a bundle of contradictions. And his outward appearance was as strange as his mind. The son of parents both noted for their beauty and gracefulness, James was shambling in gait and ugly in countenance. Mary was one of the bravest of women: her son lived in mortal terror of assassination, could never look on a drawn sword without shivering, and wore his Lincoln green doublet and trunk hose padded till they were made dagger-proof. No caricature could be odder than the reality, yet this nondescript King had a mind of his own, obstinacy and gleams of real wisdom, which made him a dangerous antagonist to all who crossed his will. George Buchanan did his best for him. He taught him abundant Latin and Greek, and tried, by means both gentle and vigorous—more often the latter—to instil the principles of civil and religious liberty into his mind. But in this last endeavour he failed. James always associated these principles with his own early Spartan training, and bore them a hearty grudge accordingly. He had a liking for Episcopacy from the first. He loved to be considered the head of the Church, and, as the Lord's Anointed, to lay down the law on all points of doctrine and practice. He found those who were ready to admit all that he claimed for himself, and to do it in language the most foolish and servile. Witness the 'Dedication to the King' prefixed to our Bibles—one of the finest pieces of English writing in existence—and remember, as you read, what sort of man he was to whom the words were addressed.

But things had hardly yet come to a crisis. There were some men in Scotland who feared God and honoured the King in quite another fashion than that which the Dedication expresses, and who were resolved to have the Church free from Royal interference. It would not be true to say that one side was all and always in the right, while the other was in the wrong. There were faults of word and deed on both sides, as we shall see. But looking back on those stricken fields, we can see that the party which Melvill led fought throughout for liberty, and it ill becomes those who enjoy the fruits of their victory to carp and sneer at them as narrow-minded fanatics. No doubt the Church often meddled with matters it had better have left alone. For example, the Assembly of 1574, being much exercised by the prevalent extravagance in dress, remitted the matter—as its manner still is—to a committee for consideration. Here is part of their report:

'First, we think all kind of broidering unseemly: all vagaries on gowns, hoses, or coats; and all superfluous and vain cutting out, striking with silks; all kinds of costly sewing, or variant hues in sarks: all kind of light and variant hues in clothing, as red, blue, yellow, and sicklike, whilk declares the lightness of the mind; . . . all using of plaids in the kirk by readers or ministers . . . all silk hats, or hats of divers and light colours; but that their haill habit be of grave colour, as black, russet, sad grey, sad brown, or serges, worsted camlet, grogram, or sicklike.'

Needless to say, this comprehensive report was received by the Assembly with enthusiasm, and passed unanimously. Nay, in their pride, the daring members added a rider to it: 'that their wives sall be subject to the same order.' The General Assembly has done many *daft* things in its time, but surely this is the daftest. History does not say how such an egregious Deliverance was received in the country at large. Doubtless, to quote the words of the Book of Esther about another decree, 'The City Shushan was perplexed.'

But the Assembly had very soon much more difficult and important work to do than the passing of such futile sumptuary laws. A cousin of the King, Esmé Stewart by name, had come from France: a brilliant and attractive man, so far as outward appearance went, but of no worth whatever. He had been brought up at the French court, the moral atmosphere of which, at that time, was deadly to almost every one who breathed it. Showy and graceful as he was, he won the boy-king's heart, and favours of all sorts were showered on him—the King finally making him Duke of Lennox and Lord High Chancellor. His foolish head was turned by all these honours, and he conducted himself with so much insolence that the anger of nobles and people began to wax fierce against him. His influence over the King increased, as he was always ready to instil into James's mind the doctrine, in its extremest form, of the Divine right of Kings to exercise absolute rule. Moreover, he was suspected of being hand in glove with the Guises, the most powerful Catholic family in France, and closely related to Mary. Catholic invasion was a very real danger so long as Philip II was on the throne of Spain, and Mary was plotting in England; and the Church grew very anxious. At length John Durie, father-in-law of James Melvill, and one of the ministers at Leith, spoke out boldly about the ruinous influence of the favourite. He very nearly paid for his boldness with his life. Even Lennox, however, could not go so far as to put him away; the worst that could be done was to forbid him to preach and send him into banishment. His action, however, emboldened others, and by a series of cleverly planned schemes —the Raid of Ruthven—James was carried away by the nobles out of the control of Lennox, and Durie was allowed to return.

When he arrived, on a warm September day in 1582, his whole congregation turned out to welcome him on Leith sands. All Edinburgh was in the streets, and as the procession, two thousand strong, with Durie in the midst, came up the Nether Bow, they bared their heads and began to sing *in full four-part harmony* the 124th Psalm in Whittingham's great version:

Now Israel may say, and that truly,
If that the Lord had not our cause maintain'd;
If that the Lord had not our right sustain'd,
When cruel men against us furiously
Rose up in wrath, to make of us their prey;
Then certainly they had devour'd us all. . .

As the magnificent melody—the 'Ein' feste Burg' of the Scottish Reformation—rang out, the whole crowd took it up and sang 'till heaven and earth resoundit', as only those sing who have been delivered as by a miracle from such 'fierce floods' and 'rage' and 'bloody cruelty' as those of which the Psalmist sang. Of what followed here is James Melvill's account:

'This noise, when the Duke of Lennox being in the town heard, and ludgit in Hie Gate, looked out and saw, he rave his beard for anger and hasted him off the town, and remained in Dumbarton at the Wast Sea, where or he gat passage, he was put to as hard a diet as he causit the Earl of Morton til use there, yea even to the tother extremity that he had usit at court. For whereas his kitching was sae sumptuous that lumps of butter was cast in the fire when it soked [grew dull], and twa or three crowns warit upon a stock of kail dressing, he was fain til eat of a maugre guse, skowdert with bear straw.'

That the danger against which the Protestants were on their guard was no imaginary one, was shown in the space of a very few years by the descent of the Spanish Armada on the coasts of Britain. Nowadays, of course, it is easy to speak of Protestant violence and intolerance, to say that in reality there was little to choose between the two sides, and that the motives behind the Reformation were selfish rather than spiritual, and political, not religious. No one familiar with the whole story will now hold a brief for all that the Reformers said and did, but to deny that they were on the side of what made ultimately for civil and religious freedom, which was then struggling for bare existence against desperate odds, that they were willing to endure exile and death for the truth, and that by them the Bible was given and the gospel preached to Scotland: to deny all this, is to be blind to the plain facts of history. If they saw their King led astray by wicked and worthless favourites, who, they had reason to suspect, were caballing with the Catholic party in France, and, seeing this, spoke strong words, and did not treat their liege lord himself with much ceremony; all honour to them for their true patriotism at a time when it was so sadly to seek in other men.

The situation was, of course, made more difficult by James's incurable dissimulation—King-craft, as he called it. His duplicity benefited him not at all, costing him endless trouble, the endurance of some uncommonly plain speaking from Melvill, and the forfeiture of the respect and confidence of all honest men. The same thing was to cost his son his head. It was utterly impossible to pin James down to his word. He would promise one thing and do another, and justified himself by his conviction that, as the Lord's Anointed, he was above all law. For example: Presbytery had been established; then another law was passed putting all matters in Church and State under the absolute control of the King and the Privy Council. Without the King's consent, Presbyteries and Assemblies could not meet. Episcopacy was re-established, and the severest restraints were put upon freedom of speech. These regulations were known as *The Black Acts*.

On 8 February 1587, in the hall of Fotheringhay Castle, Mary Stewart—'the Daughter of Debate, that eke Discord doth sowe'—ceased from troubling. Eighteen months later,

About the lovely close of a warm summer day,

the Armada was sighted, bearing up the English Channel. Through all the next night the beacons flashed the news of the coming of the Dons:

Such night in England ne'er had been, nor e'er again
              shall be.
From Eddystone to Berwick bounds, from Lynn to
              Milford Bay,
That time of slumber was as bright and busy as the day.

The brunt of the attack fell on England, but in the final repulse of the Spaniard[1] Scotland, too, bore her part. There is no need to tell over again the glorious story of the chase and fight in the Narrow seas, and of how—so the inscription on the medal struck in commemoration ran—'God blew and they were scattered.'

There is but one incident in connection with that story which must be mentioned. James Melvill was minister at that time in Anstruther, the quaint little red-roofed fishing town in the East Neuk of Fife. Early one morning, towards the end of that memorable autumn, he was awakened by one of the bailies of the town coming to his bedside. 'I have news to tell you, sir. There is arryvit within our herbrie this morning a ship full of Spainyarts, but not to *giff* mercy, but to *ask*.' The Spaniards had landed, but the prudent town-councillors had ordered them back to their galleon until they could decide what should be done with them. They had the greatest respect for the shrewdness and humanity of their minister, and would do nothing without his advice. Up got Melvill, and soon the two

---

[1] King James was characteristically occupied that winter, so Melvill tells us, 'in commenting of the Apocalypse and in setting out of sermons thereupon against the Papists and Spaniards'. Fortunately there were others in Scotland who employed their time to better purpose.

men were hurrying to the Tolbooth, passing the word as they went to the burghers to follow them. There advanced to meet them a 'valiant gentleman of Spain', Don Juan Gomez de Medina, 'grey-haired, grave, and stout of countenance', who, bowing low before Melvill, made a long statement in Spanish: how they had been driven north and wrecked on the Fair Isle between Orkney and Shetland, and after suffering terrible hardships, had at last made their way south thus far, and now sought relief for himself, his captains and soldiers, who were all in pitiful plight. Melvill assured him that though his own countrymen had been hardly used and persecuted by the Spaniards, yet they would find nothing in Anstruther but Christian pity, and works of mercy and alms, leaving to God to work on their hearts concerning religion as it pleased Him. So the Spanish seamen—'for the maist pairt young beardless men, silly, trauchled, and hungert'—were entertained hospitably by the townsfolk, to whom they made great 'Dewgard[1] and courtesy'.

Meanwhile, Spaniards and Scots alike believed that the rest of the Armada had escaped safely, until one day in St Andrews, Melvill got a broadsheet telling of the wreck of the galleons in the Hebrides and all round the coast, 'the quhilk when I recordit to Jan Gomez, by particular and special names, "O then," he cried out for grief, bursted, and grat.' It is pleasant to think that Gomez on reaching Cadiz and finding an Anstruther sloop in trouble there, straightway told his story, and put himself about to such good purpose that he got the crew off safe and sound, and sent them home with many messages to his friends the minister and laird of Anstruther.

As Professor W. P. Ker truly says, 'This meeting shows the Scottish minister hardly surpassed in grace of bearing by the Spanish general: the record of it in a few pages contains what is missed in the other contemporary documents about the Armada, perfect justice to both sides, and what is rare in any contemporary history, an adequate rendering of the best qualities of both sides. It is a passage that may be dwelt on; it clears away the turbulent accidents of history, and leaves the

[1] Dewgard, a salutation from the French *Dieu garde*.

characters by themselves, understanding one another as
honourable men, in spite even of their religions and with no
unworthy condescension on either side.'[1]

To obtain any clear idea of James Melvill, it is necessary to
read his gossiping desultory Diary. There, quite unconsciously,
he draws his own portrait, and a singularly attractive one it is.
He takes us into his confidence, giving the most intimate details about himself and his family, his dreams, his superstitions,
his feelings spiritual and physical when he went on any voyage
—these last described with a realism which leaves nothing to be
desired so far as accuracy is concerned. He introduces several
of his poems, of which he was evidently very proud, though he
modestly calls them—and with truth—'dwabbling country
rhymes'.[2] And everywhere there shine out from the pages of
the book his kindly humour, his simple faith and charity.
Again to quote W. P. Ker, 'He was not a great writer, nor
a great scholar, nor a statesman; but he is representative of
the highest ideals of the time, the energy in learning and teaching, the devotion to high aims, the interest in all things human,
the self-respect and self-sacrifice: the greater men of that age
are in many ways less representative.'[3] I shall quote two short
passages. The first describes an interview he and his uncle had
with George Buchanan in the great scholar's last illness.

'That September [1581] in time of vacans, my uncle Mr
Andro, Mr Thomas Buchanan, and I hearing that Mr George
Buchanan was weak and his History under the press, passed
ower to Edinburgh anes errand to visit him and see the wark.
When we cam to his chalmer we fand him sitting in his chair
teaching his young man that servit him in his chalmer to spell
a. b. ab; e. b. eb, etc. After salutation Mr Andro says, 'I see,
Sir, ye are nocht idle.' 'Better this,' quoth he, 'nor stealing
sheep, or sitting idle, quhilk is as ill!' Thereafter he shewed us
the Epistle Dedicatory to the King; the quhilk when Mr Andro
had read, he tauld him that it was obscure in some places, and
wanted certain words to perfect the sentence. Says he, 'I may

---

[1] Craik's *English Prose Selections*, i, 500.

[2] As a poet it must be confessed that, as was said of another Montrose
worthy, James Melvill was 'mair wullenter than qualifeeder'.

[3] Craik's *English Prose Selections*, i, 506.

do nae mair, for thinking on another matter.' 'What is that?'
says Mr Andro. 'To die,' quoth he; 'but I leave that and
many more things for you to help.' We went from him to the
printer's wark-house, whom we fand at the end of the 17th
Buik of his Cornicle at a place quhilk we thought very hard for
the time, quhilk might be the occasion of staying the haill
wark, anent the burial of Davie.[1] Therefore staying the printer
from proceeding we cam to Mr George again and fand him
bedfast by [i.e. contrary to] his custom; and asking him, how
he did? 'Even going the way of weelfare,' says he. Mr Thomas
his cousin shows him of the hardness of that part of his story,
that the King wald be offendit with it and it might stay all the
wark. "Tell me, man," says he, "giff I have tauld the treuthe?"
"Yes," says Mr Thomas, "Sir, I think sae." "I will bide his
feud, and all his kin's, then!" quoth he: "Pray, pray to God for
me, and let Him direct all!" '

The other quotation is of a very different kind and tells of his
first great grief in his life. It was in the Armada year, when his
little son Andrew died.

'The bairn was fallon beautiful, loving, and merry and seemed to be of a fine sanguine constitution, but syne his flesh and
colour failed, and by the space of a quarter of a year consumed
and dwyned away, keeping always the sweetest and pleasant-
est eye that could be in any ones heid. I was accustomed to set
him at the end of the table, in time of denner and supper as the
Egyptians did the picture of deid, til acquent me therewith,
and yet when he died, I marvelled at my ain heart that was sa
movit with it, sa that yet when I wrote this, I was nocht free
from the boundings of that natural affection. And if we that
are earthly worms can be sae affected to *our* children, what a
love bears that heavenly Father to *His*? He was my first
propyne and hansel to heaven. I can nocht forget a strange
thing at his death. I had a pair of fine milk white dowes,
quhilk I fed in the house: The ane whereof that day of his death
could nocht be halden off his cradle, but stopped from sitting
above it, crept in, and sat under it and died with him. The
other at my hame coming on the morn, as I was washing my
hands, lighted at my foot and piteously crying "Pipe, pipe,

[1] The reference is to Rizzio, Queen Mary's favourite, and so verges on the
libellous.

pipe!" ran a little away from me. . . Then I called for peas and beans to give it, but they shewed me it wald nocht eat, and parting from me with a pitiful piping within two or three hours died also. This page if thou be a father that reads it, thou wilt pardon me. If nocht, suspend thy censure till thou be a father as said the grave Lacedemonian Agesilaus. Sa the Lord taks, the Lord gives; blessed be the name of the Lord for ever!'

Both Andrew and James Melvill had at one time to flee the country because of the anger of the King. Andrew had been sentenced to ward himself in Blackness Castle,[1] whose ungainly barrack-like bulk may still be seen on the southern shore of the Firth of Forth between Queensferry and Grangemouth. He managed, however, to give his warders the slip and to reach, in safety, Berwick-on-Tweed, where King James could not touch him.

Both the Melvills, however, were suffered to return, as King James, in the words of John Hill Burton, 'had one of those erratic wills on the motion of which no one could calculate, and he might be found doing something as far off from the character indicated by his common habits as he could go'.

The 'Black Acts' already referred to were repealed, and Presbytery was again established. Then James began his curious mole-like workings once more. It was now evident that he was to be Elizabeth's successor, and there was a powerful Catholic party in England with whom he was anxious to ingratiate himself. At the same time, he went on making overtures to the Presbyterians, and thus both parties were soon in a ferment. A council was summoned to meet at Falkland (September 1595) at which there was some very plain speaking by Melvill to the King. A second time they met. The spokesman at first was James Melvill, he being more a favourite at court. He was speaking as quietly and persuasively as he could, when the

---

[1] Blackness Castle plays almost as important a part in the history of this time as Dunottar did later, and it was of it that Lady Culross the correspondent of Samuel Rutherford writing to William Rigg, a sturdy Edinburgh bailie, who had been imprisoned there for refusing to communicate kneeling, said that though his enemies might put him in the darkness of Blackness, it was beyond their power to put him into the blackness of darkness.

King interrupted him, and called the meeting of Assembly which had sent them unauthorized and seditious. Melvill still kept cool, and answered mildly, for the Church always *was* loyal albeit candid and plain-spoken to a degree unknown in other countries in those days. At last Mr Andro's temper, never very patient, gave way before the King's interruptions. At once there was a great scene, the King 'maist crabbit and colerick'.

'Andrew Melvill [his nephew goes on] calling the King but "God's silly vassal", and taking him by the sleeve, says this in effect: "Sir, we will humbly reverence your Majesty always, namely in public, but since we have this occasion to be with your Majesty in private, and the truth is, ye are brocht in extreme danger baith of your life and your crown, and with you the country and Kirk of Christ is like to wrack, for nocht telling you the truth, and giving of you a faithful counsel, we maun discharge our duty therein, or else be traitors baith to Christ and you. And therefore, Sir, as divers times before, sa now again, I maun tell you *there is twa Kings and twa Kingdoms in Scotland. There is Christ Jesus the King and His Kingdom the Kirk, whase subject King James the Sixt is, and of whase Kingdom nocht a King, nor a lord, nor a heid, but a member*. And, Sir, when ye war in your swaddling-clouts, Christ Jesus rang freely in this land, in spite of all His enemies, and His officers convenit for the ruling of His Kirk, quhilk was ever for your welfare and defence,when thir same enemies was seeking your destruction and cutting off. But if ye cleave uprightly to God, his true servants shall be your sure friends, and He shall compel the rest to give themselves and serve you as He did to David." '

These were bold words honestly spoken, and it would have been well for James had he listened to and obeyed the advice, roughly indeed but honestly and loyally given. But the house of Stewart was wise in its own conceits, and at last, in its pride by the judgement of God, it fell.[1]

---

[1] Others were not less bold than Melvill. The King caused a public scandal by persistently neglecting to bring George, Earl of Huntly, to trial for the murder of 'the Bonnie Earl of Moray'. Patrick Simpson, minister of Stirling, preaching before the King, chose for his text, the words, 'Where is Abel, thy brother?' and pointedly addressed his Majesty, saying, 'Sir, I

Meanwhile, the life of the great Queen Elizabeth was almost spent. Men used to say as they looked on her fast whitening head: 'When that snow melts, there will be a flood.' It was indeed a change when James came to the throne. He must have felt a new freedom. He was allowed far more of his own way, and found many ready enough to flatter him even to *his* heart's content. Presbyterians, Episcopalians, and Catholics all alike expected much from him, for he was deeply pledged to them all. The famous Hampton Court conference was summoned, and there it was very soon evident that he was heart and soul in favour of Prelacy. He had now the chance of paying back old grudges, and did so with interest. The Puritan party had presented a petition, but he would have none of it. Then he went on, while the bishops in their lawn purred approval at his side: 'My lords, the bishops, if once you were out, and they in place, I know what would become of my supremacy. No bishop, no King, as before I said. I shall make them conform themselves, or I will harry them out of this land or yet do worse.' Whereupon—I am quoting from the contemporary Episcopalian record—'The Archbishop of Canterbury said that undoubtedly His Majesty spake by the special assistance of God's spirit. The Bishop of London upon his knees protested that his heart melted within him with joy, and made haste to acknowledge to Almighty God the singular mercy we have received of His hands in giving us such a King as since Christ's time the like, he thought, had not been; whereunto the lords with one voice did yield a very affectionate acclamation.'[1]

James was not yet done with the Melvills. He summoned them both to London to treat with them, as he said, about

---

assure you the Lord will ask at you, Where is the Earl of Moray, your brother?' 'Mr Patrick,' answered the King before the whole congregation, 'my chalmer door was never steekit upon you; ye might have told me anything you thought in secret.' 'Sir,' replied Simpson, 'the scandal is public.' Row's *History of the Kirk of Scotland*, p. 144. Quoted by Macpherson, *Doctrine of the Church in Scottish Theology*, p. 135.

[1] To James the change from Scotland and 'Mr Andro' to Hampton Court and its complaisant bishops must have been like passing from North-East blasts of sleet to the Riviera.

'such things as would tend to settle the peace of the Church'.
Certainly, his method of carrying out this most laudable design
was singular. He first summoned them to his chapel at Hampton Court where, as Melvill pathetically says, 'We fand a place
prepairit for us hard beside the Preacher Bishop Barlow,
whome before the King, Queen, and Nobles we *patiently heard*
mak a long or well-joined sermon, written and finely-com-
pacted in a little buik, whilk he had always in his hand for help
of his memory.' Next, the King made them attend service in
his chapel on St Michael's Day, when the service was so
extremely ritualistic, that some Frenchmen who were present
said there was nothing of the Mass wanting but the adoration
of the Host, and that they did not see what should hinder the
churches of Rome and England to unite. Andrew Melvill,
when all was over, relieved his feelings in an exceedingly pun-
gent Latin epigram on the service. For the writing of this he
was summoned before the Privy Council and after several
stormy scenes there—in one of which he actually took hold of
the lawn sleeves of the Archbishop of Canterbury and shook
them 'freely and roundly, calling them "Romish rags and a
pairt of the Beast's mark" '!—was thrown into the Tower,
where Sir Walter Raleigh, another of King James's victims,
was confined at the same time. There he was kept for ten
months, allowed to see no one, and for a long time denied the
use of pen, paper, and ink—perhaps the hardest privation for a
man of his temperament. When, however, he was released, it
was found that the walls of his cell were all covered with Latin
verses, beautifully incised by the tongue of his shoe buckle!
What *could* be done with an irrepressible spirit like this? Truly
for such as he,

Stone walls do not a prison make, Nor iron bars a cage.

The truth that everything depends on the point of view is
amusingly exemplified by Izaak Walton's account in his *Life of
George Herbert* of these same transactions:

'But to return to Mr Melvill at Hampton Court Conference;
he there appeared to be a man of an unruly wit, of a strange
confidence, of so furious a zeal, and of so ungoverned passions

that his insolence to the King, and others at this conference, lost him both his Rectorship of Saint Andrews and his liberty too; for his former verses, and his present reproaches there used against the Church and State, caused him to be committed prisoner to the Tower of London: where he remained very angry for three years.'[1]

The severity of his imprisonment was afterwards relaxed. He wrote countless verses and letters, translated many of the Psalms into Latin verse during this time, and at last, after weary waiting, the order for release came. Liberty was granted him on condition of his leaving the country, and returning no more. He was invited to become Professor of Theology in the Huguenot University of Sedan, where several of his own countrymen were already on the teaching staff and so, at the age of sixty-six, Andrew Melvill began the world again, leaving Britain, never to return.

James Melvill also had been allowed liberty on condition of never returning to Scotland. He went first to Newcastle, where he was kept pretty closely, not being allowed even to see his wife, John Durie's daughter, whom he had married in youth, and who now lay on her deathbed in Anstruther. The King characteristically tried to win him over by the offer of a bishopric (as his own elegant expression on a former occasion was—'streaked cream in his mouth'), and he as characteristically refused the bribe, preferring to live in exile with a good conscience, to living in his own country with a bad one. He was afterwards allowed to go as far as Berwick-on-Tweed, and there in that ancient town by the sea—which according to the old saying and Royal Proclamations is neither in England nor in Scotland but in a realm of its own—with its red-tiled roofs and low fortifications, and among its kindly folk with their soft Northumbrian speech, the last few years of his life wore to their close. His health had been feeble for some considerable time, though, so far as years went, he was not an old man. He died as he had lived; calm, gentle, and fearless to the last; characteristically asking that the candle might be lighted before him—'that I may see to die'. Then lifting up his hands in prayer,

[1] Walton's *Lives*, p. 188.

> He gave his body to that pleasant country's earth,
> And his pure soul unto his Captain Christ,
> Under whose colours he had fought so long.

It was on the morning of Thursday, 20 January 1614.

News travelled slowly in those days, and it was not till the following April that his uncle, whom he had loved and reverenced so deeply, heard with sore grief of his death. He found his one solace in the thought that James was now 'out of all doubt and fasherie, enjoying the fruits of his suffering here'. He himself lived for eight years more, still working busily, teaching, writing, disputing; but of these closing years we know hardly anything. The end came some time in the year 1622— the exact date and the circumstances of his death being alike unknown. He was seventy-seven years of age, and, so far as we know, worked to the last and died in harness. His body lies in the churchyard of that little town in Lorraine where at last he found

> Sleepe after toyle, port after stormy seas,
> Ease after warre, death after life.

Sedan was *then* and for long years afterwards remote and obscure, but *now* is famous in every land and for all time as the place where the sixteenth decisive battle of the world was fought in 1870, when one Empire was shattered to its foundations, and another leaped into life.

I need say little more in summing up the character and work of Andrew Melvill. That character, as we have seen, was strongly marked, alike in its excellences and in its defects. It would be an injustice, however, that you should conceive him to have been a mere pertinacious and fiery disputant, fierce and narrow in his judgements of all opposed to him. Certainly, he was, according to that old Latin line—*Impiger, acer, iracundus*, which Sir Walter Scott so admirably rendered in the vernacular:

> A fiery ettercap, a fractious chiel,
> As het as ginger and as stieve as steel.

He was all that, but he was much more. One side of his character I have hardly touched upon. In a learned age he was a scholar of European fame. Those most competent to judge give the highest praise to his Latin poems, and many of his learned contemporaries and correspondents lamented that the busy life which he led prevented him from winning fame in the realm of pure scholarship. But he made his choice and for this his country is to all time his debtor. In his numerous Latin letters we find the utmost graphic power, and not only sarcasm, but a kindly humour and playfulness, which those who met the terrible Principal only in controversy, and knew the weight of his mailed fist, probably never suspected. His services to education, in the Universities of Glasgow and St Andrews, and in general stimulus all over the country, are writ large in the history of modern Scotland. Of his stern integrity, his valour for the Truth, his simple faith in God, there is no need to speak.

James Melvill lies in an unknown grave in Berwick; Andrew Melvill in Sedan. To neither, so far as I know, has any monument been raised. What need is there for one, at least in Scotland?

> Let the sound of those they wrought for,
> And the feet of those they fought for,
> Echo round their bones for evermore.

Surely, we honour these two noble men best of all, in times and conditions so different from theirs, by holding fast the same great principles of Reform and Freedom, alike in the Church and in the State, for which they fought a fight, so faithful and so valiant, three and a half centuries ago.

INDEX

137